Jesus and Paul Agree:

You Don't Have To Stay The Way You Are

Knofel Staton

A Division of Standard Publishing
Cincinnati, Ohio
40-040

Dedicated
to my closest and best friend,
who on August 17, 1963,
became my life's partner:
Julia

Library of Congress Catalog Card No. 76-26297
ISBN: 0-87239-109-4

© 1976. The STANDARD PUBLISHING COMPANY, Cincinnati, Ohio.
Division of STANDEX INTERNATIONAL CORPORATION.
Printed in U.S.A.

Preface

Pilate once asked, "What is truth?" and man is still asking that question. In fact, some Christians asked it years after Jesus said, "I am . . . the truth" (John 14:6). Jesus also said that God's Word is truth (John 17:17), but how could both be truth? Jesus was God's Word in flesh (1:1, 14). He spoke nothing without having first heard it from His Father (12:49, 50).

What happened to the truth Jesus lived and spoke after it passed through the minds of His first followers, particularly His apostles? Many people tell us that the apostles altered the truth to fit their individual ideas; therefore their writings are just opinions of men. It behooves us to ask, "Can we trust these apostles? Were they *communicating* Jesus' teachings or *changing* them?"

Paul gives us a classic example for study. In Lesson One I have presented Paul's drastic change from persecutor of Christ to persecuted for Christ. It is concluded that there could be only one explanation for such a change—his total denial of self and a total commitment to Jesus. If his life was like that, surely his letters were. In the second lesson I examine some evidences for believing that none of the New Testament writings altered Jesus' truths.

In the following lessons I look at some of the great teachings in the New Testament, to see how they are interrelated. I consider what they mean now as well as then, and whether or not Paul's teachings on these topics really square with those of Jesus.

An important question for us to ponder is whether or not *our* commitment to truth can be as solid as Paul's. There was so much in the way he was brought up, his adult environment, and his position in life, that caused him to stand across the street from where Jesus stood on issues. And that is where many of us also find ourselves. Our environment doesn't square with Jesus' enlightenment on many issues either. But what will *we* do with God's truth? Will we allow our tradition, environment, and position to cause us to say, "I can't or won't accept that"? Paul crossed the street to stand where Jesus stood, regardless of the consequences. Are we willing to do the same?

In this book we begin by viewing some of the great teachings about who *Jesus* is (Lesson Three). We end our study by looking at the great teachings about whom *we* can become (Lesson Thirteen). But we cannot jump from the beginning to the end without considering seriously the growth we can experience by knowing and applying the truths brought out in the lessons between.

God's goal for us all is that we may become like Jesus in this world (Romans 8:28, 29; 2 Corinthians 3:18; Ephesians 4:13, 14; 1 John 4:17). May we be committed to move toward that goal, and may this book lead us to both His Book and His people. Both God's Book and God's people help us to move from singing, "Just As I Am" to the position of singing, "Just As He Is."

Knofel Staton

Unless otherwise identified, every Scripture quotation is from *The New American Standard Bible and New Testament*. By permission of The Lockman Foundation, F. D. Lockman, President.

Contents

Part One: Theological Comparisons

Lesson	Page
1. Jesus or Paul?	9
2. Is the New Testament Valid?	17
3. Paul's View of Jesus	28
4. The Reality of Sin	36
5. The Two Sides of Salvation	44
6. The Holy Spirit	53
7. Law and Freedom	58
8. Love That Lives	64

Part Two: Practical Comparisons

9. Love That Breaks Down Walls	75
10. Women Then and Now	83
11. Survival of the Family	93
12. Christian Reactions	101
13. Christ's View of Greatness	107

PART ONE:

Theological Comparisons

Jesus: "The things I speak, I speak just as the Father has told Me"
John 12:49

Paul: "For I neither received it from man, nor was I taught it, but I received it through a revelation of Jesus Christ"
Galatians 1:12

For The Christian: "And the things which you have heard from me in the presence of many witnesses, these entrust to faithful men, who will be able to teach others also"
2 Timothy 2:2

Lesson One

JESUS OR PAUL?

Whom To Believe

Jesus is divine; Paul was only human. Does this mean their teachings are contradictory? Should we follow Jesus' teachings, but be cautious about following Paul's teachings? Should we disregard Paul's teachings altogether because he expressed only human (and faulty) opinions?

Some time ago I attended a Christian seminar, led by a man with a Ph.D. in counseling. He suggested that parents should not have authority over their children, for this thwarts the development of intiative in children. When a member of the class quoted Paul in Ephesians 6:1: "Children, obey your parents," the leader declared, "Oh, we can't follow Paul. One of the most important things you can learn is this: Jesus is our primary source. Paul is human. Anytime Paul disagrees with Jesus, we must ignore Paul's teaching."

The leader then referred us to Matthew 10:34-37: " 'Do not think that I came to bring peace on the earth; I did not come to bring peace, but a sword. For I came to set a man against his father, and a daughter against her mother, and a daughter-in-law against her mother-in-law; and a man's enemies will be the members of his household. He who loves father or mother more than Me is not worthy of Me.' "

"It is clear," the leader continued, "that Jesus did not intend for children to obey their parents. We should follow what Jesus said, not what Paul said."

When I challenged his remark, the seminar leader conceded that perhaps this was not the best illustration of the disagreement between Jesus and Paul. Then he had us consider Galatians 5:12: "Would that those who are troubling you would even mutilate themselves."

"This is a clear contradiction to Jesus' teachings," the leader declared. "Jesus' attitude was the exact opposite of Paul's."

The approach of this seminar leader to Scriptural teaching is a common one today. Many scholars say that Jesus brought truth, while Paul brought theology; that Jesus was the founder of Christianity, while Paul was the first innovator. Many believe that Paul was an interpreter of Jesus, but he goofed in some of his interpretations.

To believe and to teach these ideas is to call into question the trustworthiness of most of the New Testament, for Paul wrote almost one-third of the New Testament. The activities of the church would also be questioned, for much of Christianity as we read of it in the New Testament was the result of Paul's (or members of his team) evangelizing and teaching endeavors.

For instance, seventy-five percent of the book of Acts, which covers one-seventh of the New Testament, is filled with the activites of Paul. Acts traces the expansion of Christianity from a Jewish congregation in one location to a worldwide movement that included all races. If what Paul did and said are to be considered strictly human, then we have no trustworthy source for determining many important aspects of church life. If he was just an innovator, we can be innovators also, without considering his teachings or activities.

A recent book that defends "Christian homosexuality" (a mutually exclusive term) uses the approach that Jesus' and Paul's teachings are contradictory. The author states that Jesus never once spoke against homosexuality. Any reference to antihomosexuality in the New Testament is due to Paul's own private opinion and prejudice.

How can we handle such a statement? We can discover that homosexuality is certainly condemned by God in the Old Testament (Leviticus 18:22; 20:13). Considering the relationship between God and Jesus, wouldn't Jesus hate what God hates? Jesus used a word that covered all sorts of sexual perversions (translated "fornication") and condemned them all (Matthew 15:19). Jesus used a general term, while Paul was more specific in naming some of those perversions. Was Paul correct in doing so? To answer that, we must consider the relationship between Paul and Jesus. Are their teachings and attitudes contradictory or harmonious?

A Contradictory Relationship

In the beginning, Jesus and Paul were poles apart in their thoughts and attitudes. Paul was a son of Judaism; Jesus was the Son of God. They spoke from different perspectives. Jesus spoke the words of His heavenly Father (John 12:49); Paul echoed the words of Jewish tradition (Galatians 1:14). Paul was trained as a Hillel scholar under Gamaliel. The Hillels taught that a man could divorce his wife for any reason, which was no doubt Paul's position. It certainly was not Jesus' position.

Paul was prejudiced against the Gentiles and hooked on the necessity of the temple in Jerusalem. This is seen by his consent in the stoning of Stephen, who had given a speech against such prejudices (Acts 7). Jesus had neither prejudice (Matthew 8:11; 24:1, 2; John 2:19).

Paul believed that the traditions of the Pharisees were right (Philippians 3:5, 6). Jesus taught His disciples to beware of the leaven of the Pharisees (Matthew 16:6, 12). Paul wanted to destroy the church (Galatians 1:13). Jesus wanted to establish it (Matthew 16:18). Paul believed that the law made a man righteous (Philippians 3:6). Jesus taught that one's righteousness should exceed that of the Pharisees (Matthew 5:20).

The Change

Paul's attitudes and ideas changed! The chart on the next page shows the differences. What made him change so drastically? The same thing that makes any person change his ideas and attitudes—it is the conviction of who Jesus is and one's commitment to follow His teachings and example for living.

Before Paul was converted, he must have agreed with the Pharisees of his day, for he was "a Pharisee, a son of Pharisees" (Acts 23:6). He confessed, "I thought to myself that I had to do many things hostile to the name of Jesus of Nazareth" (Acts 26:9). As a true Pharisee, he thought that Jesus was not from God (Matthew 12:23, 24); that He was a sinner (John 9:24); that He was a liar (Matthew 9:3); that He was possessed of demons (12:24); that He had suicidal tendencies (John 8:22).

It is no wonder that Paul thought it was his duty to get rid of this fake. Several men already had claimed to be the Messiah and had led some of God's people astray (Acts 5:36, 37). Paul naturally felt he had to protect God's flock from the "wolves." Therefore, he was a part of Stephen's stoning (Acts 7:58). He engaged in a mission to search and destroy Christians (26:10). He even resorted to torture in order to get Christians to deny Jesus (26:11).

Then it happened! Jesus spoke to Paul in person! Dead men don't talk, so Paul knew that Jesus was alive. The resurrection that these Christians had talked about was true. Paul had been wrong all along. Paul realized his error and changed sides.

We must realize that Paul always lived out his convictions. He was nobody's yes man. He behaved

Before	After
A man may divorce for any reason.	Husbands should not put away their wives (1 Corinthians 7:11); wives are bound for the life of their husbands (1 Corinthians 7:39).
The Jerusalem temple is necessary for worship.	The body is the temple of the Spirit (1 Corinthians 6:19).
Prejudiced against the Gentiles.	There is no difference between Jew and Greek, slave and free, male and female. All are one in Christ (Galatians 3:28).
It is necessary for one to be a Jew physically.	If one belongs to Christ he is of Abraham (Galatians 3:29).
Circumcision was necessary.	Circumcision is not by the letter, but of the heart, by the Spirit (Romans 2:29).
The law made one righteous.	Righteousness is not derived from the law, but from faith in Christ (Philippians 3:9).
The church should be destroyed.	The wisdom of God is now manifested through the church (Ephesians 3:10).

as he believed. He was committed to live for God as he understood God's way. Paul's level of commitment and zeal did not change on that road to Damascus; he continued to live for God with total surrender.

But Paul's understanding did change on that road, as illustrated by the chart below. He found out who Jesus really was. He did not fight it. He did not intellectualize it away. he did not worry about the loss of prestige and position he would experience if he became a Christian. He was not only the one most likely to succeed in Judaism, he was the one who was a success: "I was advancing in Judaism beyond many of my contemporaries among my countrymen, being more extremely zealous for my ancestral traditions" (Galatians 1:14). It would be expected, then, that he would have had many second thoughts about changing his religion. But nothing stood in the way of Paul's

Before	After
Christ was a sinner.	He was without sin (Hebrews 4:15), but became sin in our behalf (2 Corinthians 5:21).
He was a liar.	The truth was in Jesus (Ephesians 4:21).
He was possessed by demons.	If one does not have the Spirit of Christ, he cannot belong to Him (Romans 8:9); lists the fruits of the Spirit (Galatians 5:22 ff).
He had suicidal tendencies.	Christ abolished death and manifested immortality (2 Timothy 1:10).

commitment. He counted all his achievements as rubbish in comparison with gaining the Messiah (Philippians 3:7, 8).

After his conversion, Paul understood Jesus fully and recorded for us the best word pictures of Christ that we have: "In Him all the fulness of Deity dwells in bodily form" (Colossians 2:9); "He is the image of the invisible God" (1:15); "He is also the head of the body, the church" (1:18); "At the name of Jesus every knee should bow" (Philippians 2:10); "Every tongue should confess that Jesus Christ is Lord, to the glory of the Father" (v. 11); "It is the Lord Christ whom you serve" (Colossians 3:24).

Do these words sound as if they would come from one who would change the intent of Jesus' teachings? *No!* In fact, Paul made it clear that he preached no other but Christ: "For I am determined to know nothing among you except Jesus Christ, and Him crucified" (1 Corinthians 2:2). In other words, Paul would not teach anything that would not agree with Jesus' teachings.

Paul's Commitment

Paul had come to believe that Jesus was the Messiah, the Son of God, and he behaved in accordance with his belief. Immediately after he was immersed into Christ for the forgiveness of his sins (Acts 9:18; 22:16), he began to proclaim that Jesus was the Son of God. He used Jewish Scriptures to prove that Jesus was the Christ the Jews had been hoping for (Acts 9:22; 17:2; 18:28). The persecutor became the persecuted (9:23, 24). Paul's commitment did not falter. He was willing to die for Jesus, as Jesus had been willing to die for him.

Paul understood that he was an apostle of Jesus, and he wrote as an apostle (check the beginning sentences of many of his writings). What is Paul claiming when he calls himself an apostle? The word was commonly used in the first century to identify a messenger, a letter, a ship, a delegation, or an ambassador. Being an apostle denoted the following: (1) the apostle was sent on a mission by another; (2) while on the mission, the apostle was under the authority of the person who sent him; (3) the apostle represented the person who gave the commission; (4) the apostle was to do and to say what was commissioned.

When Paul began a letter as "an apostle of Jesus Christ," he was making it clear that it was not just a personal letter but a divine one. He delcared that what he said was not his own, but the Lord's (1 Corinthians 14:37). The apostle Paul was inspired (1 Corinthians 2:12-16). Peter did not hesitate to equate Paul's writing with Scripture (2 Peter 3:15, 16).

Paul was careful to make sure that people understood his writing as being from the Lord. When he did not have a direct command from the Lord on a certain subject, he said so plainly (1 Corinthians 7:6, 25).

Summary

There is a continuity and harmony between Jesus' and Paul's teachings. Paul is the earliest writer about Christianity. He wrote most of his letters before any of the Gospels were written. Paul is our primary interpreter of the teachings of Jesus. His writings to the churches are grounded in the teachings of the Lord. He did not try to change or add to the teachings of Jesus so they would agree with the teachings of the churches of his day. Instead he tried to change the churches of his day to agree with the teachings of Jesus!

Paul was a man *in* Christ who lived and taught and died *for* Christ. He could say, "Be imitators of me, just as I also am of Christ" (1 Corinthians 11:1)—a worthy goal for us all.

Lesson Two

IS THE NEW TESTAMENT VALID?

In a party or a gathering of several people, have you ever tried whispering something into the ear of one person, then have that person whisper it into the ear of the next, and so on until the message had been passed to the last person in the group? If not, try it, and compare the original message with what the last person repeats as the message he heard. The larger the group of people involved, the less likely you are to recognize any part of your original message.

To make the experiment even more interesting, have the participants repeat the message without whispering, but between each repetition engage them in an activity or a discussion. You will probably be amazed at the final message that is repeated.

The words and activities in the New Testament happened nearly two centuries ago. If we cannot repeat messages accurately to one another today, then how can we know that the things we are reading in the New Testament are valid facts? As far as we know, nothing that Jesus said or did was written down until at least twenty years after Jesus died. Paul was the first person to write about Jesus. Mark, the first of the Gospels to be written, was probably not written until thirty-five years after Jesus died.

What Paul told of Jesus' earthly life is rather skimpy, though essential. From Paul's writings, we learn: Jesus was in the form of God before His birth (Philippians 2:5, 6); He descended from Abraham and David (Galatians 3:16); He was born of a woman (4:4); He had a brother (1:19); He was a teacher (Acts

20:35; Romans 15:8; Ephesians 2:7); He was meek (2 Corinthians 10:1); He considered others before himself (Romans 15:1-3); the Jews were the instigators of His death (1 Thessalonians 2:14, 15); He had a meal with His disciples on the night of His betrayal (1 Corinthians 11:24, 25); He was crucified (Galatians 3:1); He arose from the grave (1 Corinthians 15:4 ff); He was seen by many people (vv. 5-8); He ascended to the right hand of God (Ephesians 1:20).

At first glance, this information about Jesus seems hardly adequate; but think again! Paul's information followed a broad but basic outline of Christ's life, described more fully in the four Gospels, from John 1:1 (the pre-existence of Jesus) to Luke 24:50, 51 (the ascension of Jesus). How could Paul do this, since the Gospels were written *after* his epistles? One thing is clear: Paul did not copy what others had written! He reported his own testimony, what he had received from the Lord, not what another had done (1 Corinthians 11:23; 15:3; Galatians 1:11, 12 ff). He dealt with facts, not fables.

But can we be sure that Paul was accurate? After all, many years had passed between the reality of Jesus' life and Paul's letters about that life.

A Popular Answer

Some people today say we cannot trust the New Testament writings about Jesus, for they do not tell us the facts about Jesus but only about the faith of His followers. Thus the New Testament gives us the Jesus of *faith* (what people believed), not the Jesus of *fact* (what Jesus actually said and did). These doubters teach that the Christians made up stories about Jesus and that Jesus' teachings were only what the writers claimed He said and in *their* words. The Christians are said to have changed whatever they wanted to change to fit their beliefs and practices.

This is the popular approach to the New Testament in several seminaries and in the departments of religion in many universities. Not only is this approach being taught, but it is being accepted by people in denominational places of influence. Some evangelical seminaries are beginning to lean toward this kind of thinking. Chances are you have relatives who believe this way. One day your children may ask how you can answer this problem. After all, the university professor will probably have a doctor's degree. How do we fight that?

The rest of this book could be devoted to discussing the evidences for believing in the trustworthiness of the New Testament, but that is not its purpose. We can devote a few lines of reasoning, however.

What Can We Believe About the Resurrection?

The place to begin answering this is the same place the Christians of the first century began—with the resurrection of Jesus. The resurrection of Jesus is the central evidence of Christianity. By this the apostles were turned around.

After the arrest of Jesus, every one of the disciples deserted Him (Matthew 26:56). They thought their dream was all over, and it was time to run. It was the custom in the first century to award the followers of a master whatever honor or dishonor befell the master. The disciples figured it was time to break off relations with this Jesus. "We don't want to get what He is going to get!"

How can we explain, then, that within a few days they could not be quiet about this same Jesus? Peter was terrified to admit to an insignificant maiden that he even knew Jesus (John 18:17), but later the significant rulers of men could not squelch his words about this same Jesus (Acts 4). The disciples were at first terrified to whisper about Him, but later they were thrilled to shout about Him!

How could these changes take place if there were no resurrection? Some people say the disciples *expected* the resurrection and their strong expectations played tricks on their minds. They only imagined they saw Jesus. Oh, come off it! That is ridiculous! The disciples never expected a resurrection; they did not even believe the first reports that it had happened. They believed He was gone from the tomb, but they did not believe He had risen (John 20:8, 9; Luke 24:11; Mark 16:11, 13).

The angel's message to the women, "He is risen," did not bring joy, but fear (Mark 16:8). They simply did not believe it. Mary wept and wanted to know "where have they taken Him?" (John 20:11-13). Of course they were scared. They wondered if this was a plot of the Sadducees and Pharisees to drum up a false charge against them (that they had taken the body). They were sure the religious leaders sought to kill them. Just such a charge was made against the disciples (Matthew 28;11-15). They met behind closed doors (John 20:19, 26).

But Mary then saw and heard the physical Jesus (John 20:16, 17). Surely the disciples would then believe. But they did not believe her words (Mark 16:11). They believed when Jesus showed them the scars in His hands and feet (John 20:20, 25). They realized at last that He was no mirage. They talked with Him and saw Him eat (Luke 24:38-43). They saw Him perform a miracle (John 21:6), build a fire (v. 9), and fix breakfast (vv. 12, 13). Imagined figures don't do all of these things!

The risen Jesus remained on this earth forty days, performing many signs so people could believe He was alive (John 20:30, 31; Acts 1:3). Who knows how many signs He performed or for how many people? How much was He capable of doing in forty days? We don't know, but they were called "convincing proofs."

We have only a hint of the magnitude of the risen Lord's post-resurrection activities (1 Corinthians 15:5-7). Paul recorded that on one occasion Jesus appeared to more than five hundred brethren. If there were also women and children present, as was usual, there may have been more than two thousand people present. Paul wrote, "Most of them are still alive." What was his point? He was saying, "If you do not believe the resurrection, check it out. There is evidence all around us."

Christianity could not be stopped because its central message was grounded in the words, "He is risen!" Jesus did not allow them to preach this fact until after He had spent days showing himself. Afterward, with evidence abounding, He allowed them to get going with the Word.

All that would have been necessary to stop the spread of this Word would be to interrupt and challenge the messenger when he said, "Jesus is risen." No one interrupted. Why? Because there was too much evidence around.

To the Jews in Jerusalem, Peter said, "God raised Him up," and no one in that great audience challenged it (Acts 2:24). Instead, they said, "What shall we do?" (Acts 2:37). The Sadduccees were disturbed that Peter was proclaiming the resurrection (4:1, 2). Why should that disturb them when they had already spread the rumor that the body had been stolen? Because there was too much evidence of the resurrection around.

The magistrates of that day did not overrule Peter's point as hearsay when he said, "By the name of Jesus Christ the Nazarene, whom you crucified, whom God raised from the dead" (4:10). Why didn't they stop him right then? Because there was too much evidence around! Instead, they ordered him to quit talking about it (4:18). King Agrippa himself had no objection to the fact of the resurrection. Paul even suggested that the king knew about these facts (Acts 26:26).

People could deny that Jesus was the Messiah, the Son of God, but they could not put down the resurrection, any more than we can put down the fact that President Kennedy was assassinated in Dallas. Who would believe a writer who said Kennedy died of cancer? No one would believe it *now* because there are too many eyewitnesses around. Two thousand years from now, perhaps someone could get away with it, as people today are trying to talk away the resurrection.

But was Jesus *really* dead? Of course He was. The Romans never took a live person down from a cross. Jesus was not removed from the cross in secret. Many people who were accustomed to seeing dead people were there. Not only the followers of Jesus believed Him dead. The soldiers knew it (John 19:32-34).

The centurion, who was assigned to the crucifixion and who knew death when he saw it, gave testimony of His death (Mark 15:44, 45). Pilate was convinced.

People did not wrap live men in burial garments. Those in medicine today declare that the flow of water and blood from His pierced side (John 19:34) is evidence of His death.

The soldiers were not stationed at the tomb to prevent a live man from coming out, but to prevent live men from going in and stealing a dead body (Matthew 27:63-66).

Yes, Jesus was dead. That issue was never questioned in the first century. Pilate knew he could not get the rumor going that He was not really dead. There were too many witnesses around.

Christianity could not be nipped in the bud. Jesus had risen, and that resurrection put the stamp of authenticity on everything He had said and done.

But, of course, all we have is the written record of what Jesus said and did. How can we know that what was written down squares with what Jesus actually said and did?

The facts about Jesus were written down while the eyewitnesses were still alive. The facts told by those eyewitnesses spread across the whole world, for people from every nation traveled in and out of Jerusalem.

God made certain that there were eyewitnesses to most of the major events in Jesus' life—His birth, baptism, teachings, miracles, death, resurrection, and ascension. Many of the witnesses to some of those events did not believe in Him. They would have been the first to stop the early Christians from making up stories.

For instance, many of the five thousand people who were miraculously fed by Jesus walked away from Him (John 6:66), but they could not deny the facts written about that day. If it had been a fabrication, they would have said so.

Promise of Inspiration

In all of these things we have an historical, built-in check and balance system in the recording of the events of the first century. We also have the promise of Jesus that His Holy Spirit would guide the apostles into *all* the truth (John 16:13). I believe in a risen Jesus who had the power to raise Lazarus from the dead long after the lack of oxygen should have permanently damaged his brain. And, since Jesus promised to guide the apostles into *all* the truth, I will stand on what they have to say. We have no need for twentieth-century, self-claimed apostles or prophets who lay claim to additional truth. We cannot believe Jesus in John 16:13, and also believe such men. I will stick with the risen Jesus, whose death and resurrection could not be shelved.

How did the Holy Spirit guide the apostles into all the truth? By causing them to remember all that Jesus had said to them (John 14:26); and by explaining all Old Testament Scriptures that related to Him (John 15:26; 16:8-15); and that is good enough for me!

But what about those New Testament writers who did not receive that promise from Jesus—Mark, Luke, Paul, Jude, James? The answer:

(1) God inspired certain prophets in the New Testament to speak and write for Him (1 Corinthians 2:12, 13; Ephesians 4:11).

(2) What Mark, Luke, Paul, James, and Jude wrote was accepted by the apostles, who knew *all* the truth.

(3) The church is built on the foundation of these apostles and prophets (Ephesians 2:20).

(4) Paul reported that the apostles had nothing to add to his message (Galatians 2:6-9).

Jesus himself commissioned Paul to speak; God himself, through signs and miracles, put His stamp of approval upon what Paul said (Romans 15:15-20); Peter called Paul's writing Scripture (2 Peter 3:15, 16). Let us proceed to consider other evidences that support the credibility of the New Testament content.

Fulfillment of Prophecies

The Old Testament prophecies were fulfilled in the New Testament. Some have tried to weaken this point by suggesting that Jesus did not really fulfill the prophecies; He just memorized all of them and then acted them out. But how can the prophecies about Jesus' enemies be explained away? They did not even know the Old Testament. Can anyone really believe the soldiers heard that the bones of the Messiah were not to be broken, and so decided not to do it to help Jesus "play the part"? Even if I weren't a Christian, I wouldn't buy that reasoning.

Secular Information

When the New Testament speaks about points of cultural custom (wearing veils, soldier's dress, climate, weddings, etc.), it has been verified consistently by other sources. The same is true about geography (location of cities, terrain, buildings, etc.) and history (names of kings, taxes, coins, etc.). If the New Testament is consistently true about those secular and neutral matters, we can conclude that the writers were accurate reporters, on both the things we can check out and those we cannot.

No Fabrication

If the early Christians wanted to make changes to fit their beliefs, they did a poor job of it. They believed that Jesus was God in flesh, yet they write that Jesus admitted not knowing something (Matthew 24:36). Why didn't they cover up such an admission? In one instance Jesus touched a blind man twice before he was completely healed (Mark 8:23-25). Jesus was said to have been a worry to His parents. The writers said His family did not believe in Him, and even thought He had lost His senses (John 7:3-5; Mark 3:20, 21). Why didn't they tone down Jesus' words when He called the Gentiles "dogs" and Herod a "fox" (Luke 13:32; Mark 7:27)?

If the early Christian writers were recording myths instead of facts, why didn't they write that Judas repented and followed Jesus? If they wanted to show how great the apostles were, why did they allow Peter's prejudice against the Gentiles remain in the record? Why not delete his inconsistent behavior in Galatians 2? Why would they write about a church as corrupt as the Corinthian church? Why didn't they cover up the rift between Paul and Barnabas (Acts 15:36-40)?

If the Christians thirty to sixty years after Jesus lived wanted to write "scripture" to support the way they were living, our New Testament would be totally different. They would have left out or toned down many of the Lord's commands that they were having trouble carrying out. Believe me, the Sermon on the Mount would have been much easier to live out if they had changed some of those principles!

Why didn't they make such changes? Because they believed in the lordship of Jesus' words and deeds; they were inspired by the Holy Spirit; and there were too many witnesses still around who knew what Jesus taught and did.

"Beyond-the-Human" Insight

We read in Hebrews 11:3 that the things we see were made out of things invisible. How did that writer know about atoms? He did not; he was inspired! In 1 Corinthians 15:39 we read that not all flesh is alike. We used to doubt that statement. After protoplasm was discovered, scientists declared that all life was made out of the same stuff. But then we were able to look inside a cell and found out that animal cells were not the same as human cells. The Bible was right!

Miracles

The miracles that Jesus and the apostles did were God's way of telling the world, "These people are true." God had used that method as far back as Moses. When Moses complained, "They won't believe me," God gave Moses the ability to do miracles so that the people would believe him (Exodus 4:1-5). After the people believed Moses' words, he wrote the words down (24:4). Thus the Jews who did not live in Moses' day believed what he wrote.

The same is true for Jesus and the apostles. Jesus healed a crippled man, so people would know He had the power to forgive sins (Luke 5:17-24). He appealed to the people to believe in Him because of His works (John 10:38). The Bible states many times that God performed miracles to validate His messengers (Acts 2:22; Romans 15:15-19; 2 Corinthians 12:12; Hebrews 2:3, 4). Since the truth of those messengers was established in the first century, we need only their writings today.

Summary

I do not hesitate believing that the New Testament is true. It is the sword of the Spirit that convicts men of sin and righteousness. By its content, men will be judged (John 5:24; 12:48).

Let us, therefore, exercise the kind of faith that a certain soldier demonstrated. When Jesus told him that his son would be healed, the soldier believed the *word* of Jesus. He did not ask for a sign; he did not ask Jesus to come touch the boy. He simply believed His word (John 4:50).

There is no contradiction between Jesus and Paul. The same God who acted and spoke through Jesus inspired Paul. The New Testament is true whether the one speaking is Jesus or Paul. Let us consider their teachings—let us believe them, adopt them, and live them.

Lesson Three

PAUL'S VIEW OF JESUS

Paul was hooked on Jesus. He believed that in Christ he could do all things (Philippians 4:13). Yet Paul was not a spectacular person. In fact, he was inferior to others in many ways. He admits that he was sickly (Galatians 4:13, 14), that he was the least of the apostles (1 Corinthians 15:9), and that he was not a dynamic or eloquent speaker (1 Corinthians 2:1-4; 2 Corinthians 11:6).

Evidently some thought Paul looked and spoke like a weakling, for it was said, " 'His personal presence is unimpressive, and his speech contemptible' " (2 Corinthians 10:10). Don't you imagine he was quite scarred from his many beatings (2 Corinthians 11:24-28)? Quite early in his ministry, he spoke about having the "brand-marks" of Jesus on his body (Galatians 6:17). The many different environments that put stress on his body must have left him looking weatherbeaten (2 Corinthians 11:23-28; 1 Corinthians 4:11-13; Acts 9:23-25; *et al*).

But Paul did not mind. Instead, he boasted in his weakness so people could know that the powerful things which were happening in the first century were not happening because he was a superman. His personal weaknesses spotlighted the fact of Christ's power at work within him and in the world (2 Corinthians 12:9, 10).

Don't we sometimes forget that the good accomplishments in which we are involved are God's and not ours? We are the instruments, but we are not the creative power behind any good that comes. When we forget this truth, it becomes easy to substitute our own schemes for Christ's will. I just cannot imagine Paul offering a free donkey to those who brought the most visitors. Why? Because his subject was too big for that. He was not putting on a carnival act; he was proclaiming the Messiah. He wanted all the attention to be on Jesus, not himself.

Paul's commitment and methods affirmed his belief that Jesus was indeed the Messiah. Everything Paul taught and did was rooted in his understanding of the nature and role of the Messiah whom he knew to be Jesus. His high view of Jesus prevented him from entering into a low view of the ministry. But did his view square with Jesus' own teaching? Let's see.

Jesus Existed Before

At one time Paul must have agreed with those who said, "Is not this Jesus, the son of Joseph, whose father and mother we know?" But Paul no longer restricted Jesus' existence to an earthly beginning: "He existed in the form of God" (Philippians 2:6); "In Him all things were created" (Colossians 1:16); "He is before all things" (1:17). Perhaps the most startling claim of Paul about Jesus' pre-existence is found in 1 Corinthians 10:4, where Paul said that the Israelites drank from a spiritual rock which followed them in the wilderness, and this rock was Christ.

Where did Paul get those ideas? Did he imagine them? Of course not! He was inspired and taught by Christ himself (Galatians 1:12).

Jesus Was Divine

But just pre-existence was not enough; the devil also pre-existed. Paul declared (as did Jesus himself) that Jesus was and is divine.

Paul believed that when people looked at Jesus, they could see God's character. He was so convinced that Jesus was the exact representation of God's nature that he declared Jesus to be the wisdom and the power of God (1 Corinthians 1:23, 24). Paul saw the essential unity between the Father and the Son, and he communicated that unity to the churches and to us.

Paul	Jesus
"God was in Christ" (2 Corinthians 5:19).	"Even as Thou, Father, art in Me, and I in Thee" (John 17:21).
"He is the image of the invisible God" (Colossians 1:15).	"He who has seen Me has seen the Father" (John 14:9).
"For in Him all the fulness of Deity dwells in bodily form" (Colossians 2:9).	"I and the Father are one" (John 10:30).

Paul measured all his beliefs and customs by what Jesus said and did. How about us? When faced with scholarly books that claim our world evolved by accident, or when faced with the Savior who affirms the Creator God, which way do we vote?

When our culture says, "Fight back," and Jesus says, "Turn the other cheek," which do we practice? Jesus condemned divorce, but our culture glorifies it, so on which bandwagon do we jump? When your congregation has "done it that way" for a hundred years but there is no command of Jesus as to how it is to be done, how flexible are we?

When Jesus called for immersion, why do we accept substitutes? Do we regularly help *any* poor person? Just how much importance do we place on the words and works of a divine Jesus? It made all the difference to Paul. He changed job and religion and was willing to go anywhere at anytime for Jesus. How are we different?

Jesus Was Human

Paul marveled in the grand thought that He who owned the cattle on a thousand hills stripped himself of heavenly glory to put on man's body and nature; that He went to such lengths to enter into an intimate and eternal ministry for mankind. "Though He was rich, yet for your sake He became poor, that you through His poverty might become rich" (2 Corinthians 8:9). Although Paul did not provide us much detailed information about the historical facts of Jesus' life, he stressed the spiritual significance of that life and summed it up in one sentence. He was born "in order that He might redeem those who were under the Law, that we might receive the adoption as sons" (Galatians 4:5).

Paul rightly understood that Jesus condemned sin in His own flesh. Although tempted exactly as we are, He never sinned (2 Corinthians 5:21). Paul's teaching that Jesus' earthly ministry was for our redemption squares with Jesus' own teaching, "Just as the Son of Man did not come to be served, but to serve, and to give His life a ransom for many" (Matthew 20:28).

Just the fact that Jesus never sinned would not help us unless that same Jesus could live within us and help us to overcome sin. Paul taught that He can live in us and we can live in Him: "Christ in you, the hope of glory" (Colossians 1:27); "It is no longer I who live, but Christ lives in me" (Galatians 2:20); "Put on the Lord Jesus Christ" (Romans 13:14).

His teaching made it clear that there is a union of the believer with Christ and God. This was one of Paul's favorite concepts; in fact, he uses the phrase "in Christ" 164 times. But this union is not just between one individual and Jesus. To be in Christ is also to be in His body, the church. Paul said that to belong to Jesus is also to belong to everyone who belongs to Him, and that we are to cooperate in maturing in

Christ (Ephesians 4:16; Colossians 2:19). Jesus also taught and prayed about this union.

Paul knew that this union went beyond just a mystical relationship. He knew from his experience on the Damascus road that this union included the church. How did Paul know that? He was persecuting the *church,* and Jesus asked, "Saul, Saul, why are you persecuting *Me?*" (Acts 9:4). To be in Christ is to be in fellowship with the Father, with His Son, and with all His adopted sons. Jesus called His obedient followers His family.

What difference should Jesus' humanity and being in Him make to us? To Paul it made all the difference. As Christ ministered to people, so did Paul. It was not beneath Paul's dignity to ask for, collect, and deliver help for the poor in a famine-stricken area.

How are we living for Jesus? Why can't we deny verbally the sins He died to eliminate? Our so-called "Christian" country is not doing very well morally. We Christians are staying pretty quiet, aren't we?

What about the poverty in the world? Who cares that thousands die every day of starvation? How can a "Christian" publication print a picture of Indian children bloated from starvation and have the caption underneath, "The more we feed, the more they will breed"? I suspect that Paul would not allow such a publication to be printed without stating God's view in another apostolic letter.

To enjoy the union we have with Christ is to share the love, the kindness, the forgiveness, and the fellowship of Jesus. It is to allow the presence of Jesus to minister in the twentieth century as His presence did in the first century.

Bringing us into union with God was costly for Jesus. It was through the shedding of His own blood that it was possible for us to be brought near to God (Ephesians 2:13).

Jesus Died

The sacrificial death of Jesus was the biggest eye-opener for Paul. The Jews had not taught that the Messiah would die, much less die at the hands of sinful men. After all, the Messiah was the Creator. How could creatures kill Him? Their hopes rested in His coming, not in His death. What would happen to those hopes if He died, especially on a cross, which was a curse? How could anyone's life be blessed by a cursed death?

Though the Jews' conception of Messiah never included His death, Jesus kept talking about the fact that He was going to die. The Jews had to either reject Him as the Messiah or reject the fact of His death. Many Jews rejected Him as the Messiah; the disciples rejected the fact that He was going to die.

It was only after Jesus' death and resurrection that the total plan of God became clear. Christ died a *substitutionary* death. He took our sins as His own and accepted the wages. Paul gives us the best commentary on the death of Jesus: "While we were still helpless, at the right time Christ died for the *ungodly*" (Romans 5:6); "He died for *us*" (5:8); "Christ died for your *brother*" (14:15); "Christ died for *our sins*" (1 Corinthians 15:3); He "gave Himself for *us,* that He might redeem us from every lawless deed and purify for Himself a people for His own possession, zealous for good deeds" (Titus 2:14).

Paul summed up the significance of Jesus' death when he said, "There is one God, and one mediator also between God and men, the man Christ Jesus" (1 Timothy 2:5). This is precisely what Jesus meant when He said, "I am the way, the truth, and the life; no one comes to the Father, but through Me" (John 14:6).

Is the death of Christ as significant to us as it was to Paul and Jesus? Then our evangelistic zeal and missionary budgets ought to reflect it. Do we secretly believe that all those who have never heard of Jesus will be saved anyway? Won't God save the pagans who are worshiping the only gods they know? Why should we mess up their culture by preaching Christianity? We must never forget that Christ is the *only* mediator, and salvation is *only* through Him.

Are we treating our brothers in Christ as though we really believed that Christ died for them? Do we even like our brothers? Is there a Christian person whom you just can't stand? What are you doing about it?

If we really believe that Jesus reconciles us through the cross, then why do we stay angry at one another? What right do we have to partake of the Lord's Supper, if we have not settled a dispute with a Christian brother or sister? (See 1 Corinthians 11:17-22).

Why do we spread gossip, and why do we enjoy it? Why are we jealous when another drives up in a new car, gets a raise, or gets his picture in the paper? If we are truly reconciled to God, then we need to live like it.

Jesus Arose

Jesus never intended to remain in the grave. He prophesied His resurrection more than a dozen times. The resurrection was witnessed by many, including Paul, to whom it became a central doctrine (see Lesson Two).

Jesus Will Come Again

Paul's understanding of Jesus included another coming. From one of his earliest letters (1 Thessalonians) to one of the latest (2 Timothy), he spoke of Jesus' second coming.

He said Jesus was coming as a thief in the night, so we should be alert and continue to build up one another (1 Thessalonians 5:10, 11). We must not get careless or just sit around doing nothing (2 Thessalonians 3:10, 11). He will come with the angels and with those Christians who have previously died (1 Thessalonians 4:14). Those who are still on earth will unite with Christ and always be with Him (4:17). We will receive our reward (2 Timothy 4:8).

Paul warns that since that day is certain, we should engage in church discipline so people will be ready (1 Corinthians 5:5). The reunion will cause us to rejoice and be proud of those saved ones we know and with whom we have ministered (2 Corinthians 1:14).

On that day Jesus will be glorified, and the believers will marvel in Him (2 Thessalonians 1:10). This will be the day when Jesus, the bridegroom, consummates the marriage with His bride, the church (Ephesians 5:27). For that day we hope, and we have evidence for that hope. Jesus promised that day would come, and His resurrection supports that promise.

Summary

Paul's understanding of the Messiah covered the whole range from Christ's pre-existence to His second coming. In fact, Paul went even beyond the second coming when he declared that to Christ belongs eternal dominion (1 Timothy 6:16). Jesus will reign forever and ever; those in Him will reign with Him.

Considering the total scope of Christ—past and future—Paul could declare, "Therefore, my beloved brethren, be steadfast, unmovable, always abounding in the work of the Lord, knowing that your toil is not in vain in the Lord" (1 Corinthians 15:58).

Let us get as hooked on Jesus as Paul was and commit ourselves to understanding the significance of Jesus, His nature, and all that He did. Let us believe it and may our behavior demonstrate that belief.

Lesson Four

THE REALITY OF SIN

A few moments before I sat down to begin writing this chapter, I made a pot of coffee. With a fresh cup in my hand, I spent a few moments chatting with my wife. Noticing an uncomfortable look on her face, I asked if she were not feeling well.

"Oh, it's just the smell of that coffee," she said. (She doesn't drink it.) "It nauseates me."

"I'm sorry," I replied.

"It's not your fault," she said kindly.

"What do you mean, it's not my fault?" I challenged jokingly. "I caused both situations. I made the coffee and I'm responsible for your condition." You see, my wife was seven months pregnant. She had kindly shifted the responsibility away from me.

Isn't it easy to use the shifting of responsibility approach in facing the reality of sin in our lives? There seems to be something about our subhuman nature that lures us either to ignore the presence of sin or to ignore our involvement in it. Thus we become insensitive to the reality of what is happening around us, in us, and by us. The longer we remain in that ignorance the more hard-hearted we become, and the less open we are to change.

I am afraid we Americans are developing a national ignorance concerning the reality of and responsibility for sin. Recently a special grand jury in our county handed down twenty-three indictments. Every person pleaded "not guilty." I wonder how many of these pleas matched the reality. What American can forget all the denials of guilt in the matter of Watergate?

A friend of mine who is a highway patrolman in Iowa is full of stories of how people get themselves off the hook. One case is especially worth pondering. My friend had arrested a boy for reckless driving. At the trial the boy's lawyer, pointing to the "defendant," asked my friend, "Is this the boy you arrested?"

"Yes, it is," the trooper replied.

The lawyer then asked for the case to be dismissed, for the boy the trooper had identified was not the boy who had been arrested, but was his identical twin brother. The lawyer and the parents had dreamed up this neat little scheme for dodging responsibility.

Oh, this is an extreme case, you say? Is it really? How about you and me? Do we have a "twin brother" that we like to substitute for the real thing in order not to face the reality of sin in our lives? Let us look at this issue seriously and honestly.

What Is Sin?

First let us consider what sin is not. For the best possible demonstration of what sin is not, let us look at what Jesus said and did. All that made up His life was without sin. He was tempted many times, but He did not sin (Hebrews 4:14, 15).

We may be shocked as we learn the truth of what sin is not: It is not sin to work on the "Sabbath" (John 5:15-17; Mark 2:27, 28); it is not a sin to leave a worship service to be reconciled to a brother (Matthew 5:23, 24); it is not sin to be tempted (Matthew 4). It is not sin to allow people to see your good deeds (5:16); it is not sin to give honor to a human being who has served the Lord well (11:7-11); it is not sin to take the time to care for people's physical needs (25:31 ff).

It is not sin to spend time with the people who do not have good reputations (Luke 15:1, 2); it is not sin to cross the racial barrier in personal care (Mark 7). It is not sin for us to care for aged pagents with our finances (Matthew 15:1 ff); it is not sin to fellowship and worship with people who do not understand all Biblical truths exactly the way you do. (If so, Jesus could have had no worship experiences with any of the disciples).

What, then, is sin? Sin is *lawlessness* (1 John 3:4). When we desire to "do our own thing," in opposition to the Lord's commandments and will, it is sin. It is an attitude of disobedience. The "playboy" philosophy, which is so much a part of our culture, is sin. Sin is to reject God and live just to please oneself. Sin is rebellion against any restraints or control.

The first sin sprang out of a desire to cut the apron strings from God, to grow up and be independent. Such independence is sin. The statement, or philosophy, "Nobody tells *me* what to do," is too much in the world and the church. Out of this arises violent reaction against law and order.

This philosophy is too much in our homes. Too many husbands and wives find that they can live independently of each other. When they do, they do not live for one another, but for self. The current fad of drawing up contracts listing what each mate will do in a marriage is the opposite of love, for love is the giving of oneself to the other. This kind of selfish strategy always weakens the ability of the two people to be committed to each other. It usually means that the children will grow up with the same individualistic values.

Rebellious independence is seen too much at work. Who really wants a boss? When management is against labor, and labor stands against management, neither side wants to compromise or cooperate.

Our mass media (especially television) glorifies lawlessness. Physical violence brings rebellion to its most visible platform: "If the guy disagrees, get rid of him."

The corporateness of our society is weakening. The reason? Sin (lawlessness), independence from God and others. Just consider how neighborly your neighborhood is these days!

Jesus put it this way: " 'Because lawlessness is increased, most people's love will grow cold' " (Matthew 24:12); " 'Depart from Me, you who practice lawlessness' " (7:23). Paul said, "What partnership have righteousness and lawlessness?" (2 Corinthians 6:14).

All *unrighteousness* is sin (1 John 5:17). Unrighteousness means injustice. Lawlessness will always lead to injustice, because one who is independent from God and others is insensitive to the needs of others. Therefore he will be callous to the justice due them. Injustice is doled out when we lose our sense of duty in serving God and others. We are to love others (Matthew 22:36-40), and love does no wrong to another, either by intent or neglect (Romans 13:8-10). Love considers the interests of others (Philippians 2:4). Love does not live for self but for the good of others (Romans 15:1-3).

Unrighteousness is doing what is wrong and is selfish, seeking *self's* ambitions; righteousness is doing what is right, unselfish, and seeking *God's* ambitions. Jesus said, " 'He who speaks from himself seeks his own glory; but He who is seeking the glory of the one who sent Him, He is true, and there is no unrighteousness in Him' " (John 7:18). Paul warned that God will render to each person according to his deeds, "To those who are selfishly amibitious and do not obey the truth, but obey unrighteousness, wrath and indignation" (Romans 2:8).

Sin is also *failure to do what you know is right, or good* (James 4:17). "Right" is from the Greek word for "good." We may think we can be free from the responsibility of sin if we do not know what is the good thing to do. But, my friends, we cannot get off that easily. We are held responsible for determining and knowing what is right and good (Romans 1:18, 19; 2:14, 15).

Since Jesus came, we have no excuse for our sins. Jesus said it himself: "All who are in the tombs shall hear His voice, and shall come forth; those who did the good deeds, to a resurrection of life, those who committed the evil deeds to a resurrection of judgment" (John 5:28, 29). Paul agreed: "For we must all appear before the judgment seat of Christ, that each one may be recompensed for his deeds in the body, according to what he has done, whether good or bad" (2 Corinthians 5:10).

Yet we continue to try to rationalize away our failure to do good by using our "twin brother" substitute. The "twin brother" approach can work two ways. In the first way, people who are basically immoral may deny the reality of their sin by hiding it behind good deeds. They may care for their aged parents, care for others' physical needs, cross the racial barrier, spend all day on the "Sabbath" doing good, and then feel that these good deeds cover up any guilt for the immoralities they commit, such as adultery, stealing, lying, etc.

In the second way, people convince themselves that they are morally good (do not lie, cheat, kill, commit adultery, etc.); therefore they do not have to be busy meeting others' needs. They can stay in their own private shell away from the doings of others and be kept free of sin. They need not be "involved" in any but their own affairs.

If purity is defined by doing nothing (either bad or good), the cemetery ought to be the purest place around. Christians would surely be—in a sense—walking graves, if they merely stayed away from the bad but did no good.

The Effects of Sin

There is hardly a sin that does not affect if not hurt others. Mankind is so interrelated that one man's sin affects others in a "falling domino" fashion. Sadly, often the effect on others is not apparent until it is too late.

The Bible teaches that the existence of sin in the world keeps nature in a state of imbalance, so that all of the tragedies and sicknesses that we label "natural" are present because there is sin in the world. In that sense, we all are born into sin, that is, into an environment in which sin exists and the consequences of it are all around us.

In the beginning, there was interrelated harmony within all of God's creation. In the Garden of Eden (God's community of unity) no creature was a threat to another. There was no competition, but cooperation. When one portion of God's creation (man) rebelled, the whole creation was thrown out of balance because of sin.

> "The community (common oneness) was destroyed. Man began to live for self and would even kill to get his own way (Genesis 4). Man went wild, and so did the animals. Vegetation was threatened by weeds and thorns. Diseases came when the perfect balance of God's creation was upset by man's decision to be autonomous.
>
> "The Bible is clear that all of creation has been subjected to a bondage of decay and is itself waiting for its liberation from the imbalance. Liberation comes to the whole creation as man lives as a son of God and not as a god himself. (Study Romans 8:18-25.)"[1]

Sin also causes guilt, and guilt is damaging to us. Guilt cannot be covered up or shelved, no matter how many devices we use to do so. Denial of guilt,

---

[1] Knofel Staton, *How To Know the Will of God*, (Cincinnati: Standard Publishing, 1976), p. 79.

doing good deeds, blaming others, escaping through drugs or alcohol, running away—all these are futile. After all the running and the trying, the guilt is still there.

Psychologists and medical doctors are telling us now that many physical disorders we suffer are the direct results of unforgiven guilt. Guilt creates a barrier between a person and God, between a person and others, between a person and nature, and even keeps a person from liking himself.

Carl Menninger, a world-renowned psychiatrist, dropped a bombshell upon the field of psychiatry with his book, *Whatever Happened to Sin?* In this he rightly attributes the chaos of our culture to the presence of sin.

Sin needs to be forgiven, but it can never be forgiven as long as we run away from admitting that we have sinned. Sin is universal. The apostle John wrote, "If we say that we have no sin, we are deceiving ourselves, and the truth is not in us" (1 John 1:8). Paul taught that "all have sinned" (Romans 3:23). He also said that sin enslaves (6:16). The longer we deny sin, the tighter its grip is upon us. The more we try to "save ourselves" by painting good pictures of ourselves, the less we will see the need for a Savior and Lord of our lives.

We must realize that sin kills; it brings death. Sin changes what God intended one's self to be. It enslaves one to a life that is not related to the image and likeness of the life of God. The humanity that God created becomes subhuman. We become less than the persons we were meant to be. To be in this situation is to be dying spiritually.

Paul expressed this thought when he referred to those outside of Christ as being living dead men (Ephesians 2:1, 2). They were excluded from the life of God because they were ignoring reality (4:18). Such independence caused them to become callous.

In that state they could easily give themselves over to immorality, to practice every kind of impurity and greed (v. 19).

Summary

Sin is lawlessness, or disobedience, growing out of a desire and will to be independent. Sin is real and universal. We are all guilty and responsible for our sins. We cannot ignore sin, wish it away, or cover it up with good deeds. We cannot get around the responsibility for sin by pleading ignorance.

One person's sin affects other people as well as himself. In fact, all nature is affected by the fact of man's sin. The most severe truth in regard to sin is that it kills us spiritually by separating us from God. As long as we are in its grasp we are "living dead men."

The grip of sin can be released, but only as we die to selfishness in order to live for God. That is where salvation begins.

Lesson Five

THE TWO SIDES OF SALVATION

Ten years before I entered Bible college, I was a control tower operator. It was a very satisfying profession. It was satisfying to me because my objective was the same as that of the pilots: to have each plane reach its destination safely.

I remember well some anxious moments in that control tower. Many lives were endangered when planes became lost and low on fuel. Some of those planes and passengers were saved. Others were not, simply because time ran out. The pilots had waited too long to ask for help.

Many people are like that in life. It is not easy to ask for help unless one knows for sure he is lost. Even then, he may flounder around like a lost pilot, thinking he can find out where he is and can get himself out of the mess. I have known war pilots who did that and found themselves deep into enemy territory.

As in flying, so it is in faith. Some people can get far into the devil's territory without realizing it, and by then it is too late.

I have known pilots who were killed because they "felt" that the instruments were wrong. This is more likely to happen when a pilot is in the clouds. It is common for a pilot with this "feeling" to fly straight into the ground. His instruments tell him accurately what he is doing, but all his "feelings" tell him he is doing all right. He is sure that his feelings are correct and the instruments are wrong. Trusting his feelings instead of electronics is fatal.

I often wonder if many of us think and act the same way as we are heading toward our eternal destiny. Our Lord is a wonderful controller who wants us all to reach our eternal destiny safely. He already has decided what He wants our destination to be, and His goal and ours should be the same. Paul put it this way: "He chose us in Him before the foundation of the world, that we should be holy and blameless before Him. In love He predestined us to adoption as sons through Jesus Christ to Himself, according to the kind intention of His will" (Ephesians 1:4, 5).

There is no need for us to be disturbed about this idea of predestination. It simply means that God has decided ahead of time the goal He wants for us, and He has made it possible for us to achieve that goal. Predestination does not mean precoercion. God will not force us to achieve that goal. Jesus illustrated that fact in His parable of the prodigal son (Luke 15:11-32). Since "before the foundation of the world" God has never changed His mind about the kind of future He wants mankind to enjoy.

This is something like the commitment of a control tower operator. I started at O'Hare Airport in 1961, but nine years earlier I already had decided the goal I wanted for all the planes I directed. I did not change that goal when I came to O'Hare; I just continued to be committed to it.

At the same time, as much as I wanted all planes to reach their destinations safely, I could not make them do so. I could give instructions that would insure safety, but in each case the final choice was the pilot's. The pilot is the captain of his plane; he may accept or reject the controller's instructions. The bond of trust between the controllers and the pilots prevent rejection of those instructions and the resulting calamities. It is much the same between God and His people. God's instructions are for our good, but each of us is the captain of his soul. Each one can accept or reject God's instructions.

A relationship of trust is necessary. I believe we

use the wrong approach in presenting salvation to someone, when we begin by trying to argue him into a decision. The place to begin is to share with him the trustworthiness of God. God is dependable and true. God is committed to act for our good, which He did quite visibly in the coming of Jesus.

Paul said that God chose us in Christ to be holy and blameless before Him, predestining us "to adoption of sons *through* Jesus Christ to Himself" (Ephesians 1:5). Only in Christ do we reach an eternal destination safely, i.e., without condemnation.

The Need for Salvation

Outside of Christ, man is lost, regardless of how secure he "feels." This is because sin separates us from the life of God (Isaiah 59:2). When God created man, He shared with man His own life (Genesis 2:7). But when man sinned, the internal union of man and God was replaced by alienation. No longer was God in man, and no longer was man abiding in God.

Paul describes it as being "excluded from the life of God" (Ephesians 4:18). To be excluded from the life of God is to become less than what we were created to be. We no longer have the Father-son relationship. Jesus spoke of the severance of that relationship when He said to the Jews, "You are of your father the devil" (John 8:44). Paul spoke of the same when he said, "You were at that time . . . without God" (Ephesians 2:12). Paul describes this condition as "death" (Romans 6:23). How can man be delivered from this death?

God's Side of Salvation

God's grace is the answer. He sent Jesus to bring us into a reunion with the life of God. "When we were enemies, we were reconciled to God by the death of his Son, much more, being reconciled, we shall be saved by his life" (Romans 5:10; KJ). This *new life* is what Christianity is all about! This newness of life is available to the sinner only in Jesus. Jesus said, "No man cometh unto the Father, but by me" (John 14:6; KJ).

How does Jesus give us this new life? By taking our death to himself. When "death" is moved out, so to speak, we have "room" for God's life to move in. Let us consider what Jesus and Paul have to say about the process:

Jesus	**Paul**
"For the bread of God is that which comes down out of heaven, and gives life to the world" (John 6:33).	"We were reconciled to God through the death of His Son, much more, having been reconciled, we shall be saved by His life" (Romans 5:10).
"For this is the will of My Father, that every one who beholds the Son, and believes in Him, may have eternal life" (John 6:40).	"The wages of sin is death, but the free gift of God is eternal life in Christ Jesus our Lord" (Romans 6:23).
"I am the way, and the truth, and the life" (John 14:6).	"Our Savior Christ Jesus, who abolished death, and brought life and immortality to light" (2 Timothy 1:10).
"This is eternal life, that they may know Thee, the only true God, and Jesus Christ whom Thou hast sent" (John 17:3).	"That . . . Jesus Christ might demonstrate His perfect patience, as an example for those who would believe in Him for eternal life" (1 Timothy 1:16).

The promises involved rotate around the death and resurrection of Christ:

Jesus	Paul
"The Son of Man did not come to be served, but to serve, and to give His life a ransom for many" (Matthew 20:28).	"Christ Jesus, who gave Himself as a ransom for all" (1 Timothy 2:5, 6).
"For this is My blood of the covenant, which is to be shed on behalf of many for forgiveness of sins" (Matthew 26:28).	"In Him we have redemption through His blood" (Ephesians 1:7).
"I came forth from the Father, and have come into the world; I am leaving the world again, and going to the Father" (John 16:28).	"His Son, who was born of the seed of David according to the flesh, who was declared with power to be the Son of God by the resurrection from the dead" (Romans 1:3, 4).
"I am the resurrection and the life; he who believes in Me shall live even if he dies" (John 11:25).	"Since by a man came death, by a man also came the resurrection of the dead. For as in Adam all die, so also in Christ all shall be made alive" (1 Corinthians 15:21, 22).

Why was Jesus' death necessary for God's life to be renewed in us? Paul answers this in 2 Corinthians 5:21: "He made Him who knew no sin to be sin on our behalf, that we might become the righteousness of God in Him."

God allowed Jesus to die a sinner's death, even though Jesus had never sinned, as an invitation for us to lay our sins on Him. Christ died our death for us. For the person in Christ, there is no condemnation; but unless we lay our sins on Him, we will die in our sins (John 8:21).

Just as a pilot who is overly confident, one may feel he is not quite lost yet. But we cannot trust our feelings. We should trust God's reliable instruments who say, "All have sinned" (Romans 3:23). Then let us keep tuned in to Him for our directions.

Man's Side of Salvation

Paul writes, "By grace you have been saved through faith" (Ephesians 2:8). We believe that it is God's grace that saves us, through our faith in Jesus Christ. We acknowledge or confess Jesus is Lord because we believe that He is the Christ, the Son of the living God. What we believe expresses itself in what we do, so this confession also means that we will from now on be His servants.

Jesus cannot be our Savior from our sins until He becomes the Lord of our lives. When we are "baptized into Christ" (Galatians 3:27), we are baptized into His death (Romans 6:4). Thus we are "freed from sin and enslaved to God" (6:22). It is here that we bury the life that is "dead to sin" and rise to walk with Jesus in His "new kind of life." As He transferred our sins to himself in His death for sin, He transfers the new life of God to us in our death to sin (6:4). When our old selves are crucified with Him, we are no longer slaves to sin (v. 6), but servants of righteousness (v. 18).

Ever wonder why some people live the same way after they are baptized as they did before? They did not reckon or consider themselves dead to their old, selfish ways. Without this death there is no room for God's life to come in. When we trust Jesus and become His servants, changes will take place within our lives.

Let us be certain that the teachings of Paul coincide with those of Jesus concerning salvation:

Jesus	**Paul**
"This is the will of My Father, that every one who beholds the Son, and believes in Him, may have eternal life" (John 6:40).	"Believe in the Lord Jesus, and you shall be saved" (Acts 16:31).
"Repentance for forgiveness of sins should be proclaimed in His name to all the nations" (Luke 24:47).	"God is now declaring to men that all everywhere should repent" (Acts 17:30).
"Every one therefore who shall confess Me before men, I will also confess him before My Father who is in heaven" (Matthew 10:32).	"If you confess with your mouth Jesus as Lord, and believe in your heart that God raised Him from the dead, you shall be saved" (Romans 10:9).
"Go therefore and make disciples of all the nations, baptizing them in the name of the Father and the Son and the Holy Spirit" (Matthew 28:19, 20).	"And now why do you delay? Arise, and be baptized, and wash away your sins, calling on His name" (Acts 22:16).

All of these aspects are important. No one has the right to eliminate any one of them, or to "pick and choose." I am reminded of a story my third-grade teacher told us. It illustrates the importance of paying attention to complete directions:

A mother bird was explaining to her little birds how to build a bird nest. "First," she said, "you must get straw (one birdie flew away); second, you must get mud (another birdie flew away); third, you must find a safe place." The third birdie then flew away. Each birdie thought it knew how to put a nest together, but only the third one was able to apply all the directions of the mother and end up with a nest.

Results of Salvation

1. *A new life is ours.* This is the life of God's Spirit who is the abiding presence of the Father and the Son within us. This Spirit of life within enables us to live out the character of God amid the culture of men.

2. *We are new persons.* Jesus said that this is being "born again" of water and the Spirit (John 3). Paul said we are new creatures in Christ (2 Corinthians 5:17). The new self is created in righteousness, in the likeness of God (Ephesians 4:24).

3. *We are in a new position.* We are now in Christ because we have put Him on (Galatians 3:27). We are now the adopted children of God (Romans 8:15). We are now fellow citizens with all the saints and are members of the household of God (Ephesians 2:19). We are now the temple of God's Holy Spirit (1 Corinthians 6:19); we are now God's servants (Romans 6:22).

4. *We have a new purpose.* We will now serve God. We no longer live for ourselves, but for Him (2 Corinthians 5:15).

5. *We are in a new process.* When the process of conversion is completed, the process of growth begins, growth toward maturity in Christ (Ephesians 4:11-16). We can grow into His likeness because we are now freed to become what God intends us to

be—conformed to the image of His Son (Romans 8:29).

The benefits of being in Christ are broader than just life after death. Our total being is affected. Physically, we can be healthier; socially, we can get along with others better; psychologically, we will understand ourselves better; and spiritually we will be at peace with God. Paul expressed it this way: "Bodily discipline is only of little profit, but godliness is profitable for all things, since it holds promise for the present life and also for the life to come" (1 Timothy 4:8).

Summary

Salvation is not granted because of our works, but is granted to produce good works. It is God's gift to us, as both Jesus and Paul stressed. It is a love gift to be received, not a payment that is earned. We do not and will not ever deserve it. As someone has aptly put it, "God's grace is His giving us what we do not deserve; His mercy is His not giving us what we do deserve." Let us thank God for His gift and live lives of worship because of it.

Lesson Six

THE HOLY SPIRIT

Until recently we had two cars, both of which had nearly 150,000 miles on their engines. One was thirteen years old, the other, six. The six-year-old car was looking rather weather-beaten. It needed a new engine and a new paint job, so I traded it in. Now, if I had decided to keep that car for a few more years, which should I have spent money on, a new paint job or a new engine? Of course, I would choose a new engine, because it would put new life into the car.

Wouldn't it have been a shame if a good friend had put a new engine in that car without my knowing about it? It would have had a new engine, but I would be treating it like an old one. I would be afraid to take a long trip in it. I would not leave it out in the cold weather, etc. With a new engine, I would not have to take these precautions.

This illustration can be applied to a discussion about our Christianity. We have been told that our sins are forgiven, but no one told us that God had dropped a "new engine" into our lives. Not realizing this, some people naturally would expect to live their lives after baptism with the same anxieties that they experienced before baptism.

This feeling is understandable. After all, we look much the same after baptism as before. If we go into the baptistery twenty pounds overweight, we will come out of it twenty pounds overweight. If we go in with gray hair, we will come out with gray hair. The "paint job" will be the same, but we will be different inside!

While one extreme is to keep the old paint job

and have a new engine without knowing it, the other extreme is to have a new paint job but an old, worn-out engine inside. Some people have put on a new look that appears to be the new life, but they really do not have it. Sometimes this happens in highly emotionally-charged religious activities. When the cosmetics of the emotion wears off, the sap of the life is gone. This is not always true, however. We must not think Christianity is to be drained of emotion. It is not.

The New Life

The new life in Christ is the life in the Holy Spirit. In our evangelizing, we must let people know that God not only takes something away (sins), but He also adds something to our lives (His Spirit). Our sins are forgiven, so we can receive the Holy Spirit at *that time*. It is the presence of this Spirit in us that raises us to a new life, reconciles us to God, unites us with other Christians, equips us to live with God's character, strengthens us in this life, and resurrects us to the next life. Let us consider the Holy Spirit in detail.

The Promise

When we are full of sin, we are alienated from God and from His Holy Spirit. God has promised through the prophets to put His Spirit within us (Ezekiel 36:27). Jesus again offered that promise when He spoke to Nicodemus: "Unless one is born of water and the Spirit, he cannot enter into the kingdom of God" (John 3:5). To the woman at the well He said, "Whoever drinks of the water that I shall give him shall never thirst; but the water that I shall give him shall become in him a well of water springing up to eternal life" (4:14).

To the Jews attending a feast Jesus said, "If any man is thirsty, let him come to Me and drink. He who believes in Me, as the Scripture said, 'From his innermost being shall flow rivers of living water'" (7:37, 38). What is that water? The next verse explains: "But this He spoke of the Spirit, whom those who believed in Him were to receive." That verse also says that the Spirit had not yet come, because Jesus was not yet glorified.

Jesus' death, burial, resurrection, and His ascension to the Father after His resurrection, were absolutely necessary for the coming of the Spirit. Why? Because the Spirit cannot reside within a person until his sins have been forgiven. Jesus died for the forgiveness of those sins (Matthew 26:28). He was raised again for our justification (Romans 4:25); and the Spirit would not come to us until Jesus ascended (John 16:7).

With the ascension, God gave Jesus the authority to give the Holy Spirit to those who would live and die for Him. Thus Jesus told His disciples to go to Jerusalem and wait for the promise to be fulfilled (Acts 1:4). The ascension was Jesus' restoration to the throne (Matthew 19:28; John 17:5; Acts 2:30; 7:56). Peter connected it with the coming of the Holy Spirit (Acts 2:33).

Paul also understood that the Holy Spirit was promised and that Jesus' death was necessary for the Spirit to take up residence in men (Galatians 3:13, 14; Ephesians 1:13).

The Person of the Holy Spirit

The Holy Spirit is the extended earthly presence of God and Christ in us. Jesus made this clear in His discourse after the last supper (John 14-17): "'I will ask the Father, and He will give you *another Helper,* that He may be with you forever'" (14:16). "Another" in Greek means another of exactly the same kind, the same kind as Jesus. The word "helper" is clearly referred to in verse 26 as the Holy Spirit. In 1 John 2:1, the word is translated "advocate," and clearly refers to Jesus. These verses show the close connection between the Holy Spirit and Jesus!

Jesus further tightened up this connection when He said, "If anyone loves Me, he will keep My word; and My Father will love him, and We will come to him, and make Our abode with him" (John 14:23). "We" in this verse refers to Jesus and the Father. How can they make their dwelling place in those who love them? Through the Holy Spirit!

Paul also understood the close connection between the Holy Spirit and the presence of God and Christ in us. He spoke of the Spirit as being the Spirit of God *and* Christ (Romans 8:9). He also connected the "Spirit of God" with the "mind of Christ" (1 Corinthians 2:14, 16). He spoke of Christ being in us and God being in us (Colossians 1:27; Philippians 2:13).

There can be no mistake. The bodies of Christians house the presence of God. He is the new life we have within us. We are raised from baptism with that new life. God is at work within us. Let us be certain we teach this truth.

The Productivity of the Holy Spirit

Since God is at work in us, we have equipment after baptism that we never had before. The "paint job" may be the same, but the "engine" is new. Therefore, we must not think we are like the same old car, or still enslaved to sin. We are not. God's Spirit has moved in. This does not mean we will never be tempted again, but we no longer have to yield to the temptation as we did before. We now have a "Helper" living inside us.

Some people continue to sin after their baptism because they have never considered themselves to be different. We are different, nevertheless, and sin is not to reign within us anymore (Romans 6:12). God's characteristics are now alive in us, desiring to grow and develop. Love, joy, peace, patience, kindness, goodness, faithfulness, gentleness, and self-control are all inside us wanting to become our habitual lifestyle.

When we become Christians, we are born again. We are as newborn spiritual infants, seeking to grow and develop into Christ's image. The Holy Spirit strengthens us for that kind of growth (Ephesians 3:16). This developmental process takes time and requires provisions from God and actions from us.

Provisions of the Holy Spirit

To grow into the measure of Christ, every Christian must use his God-given abilities for others (Ephesians 4:11-16). God holds us together by what each person has to contribute to the other. With our new life in the Spirit, we contribute whatever abilities we have (Ephesians 4:16; Colossians 2:19).

The church is like a body, in that many members make it work, even though each member has a different function (Romans 12:4-8). God gave us these unique differences (1 Corinthians 12:1-27) and unites us amid those differences. In this way the different needs of the various members can be met with the use of diversified gifts (abilities).

These truths should enable us to work with cooperation, not with competition. Some people may have more "spectacular" abilities than others, that is, more prominent or seen more in public. But in the church there must be no inferior or superior feelings (1 Corinthians 12:14-17). Everyone is a someone in Christ's body. Everyone is needed. Let us reach out and help one another! That's what it means to live in the Spirit.

Lesson Seven

LAW AND FREEDOM

Have you ever felt that you would like to live for God, but you just couldn't? There was a time in Paul's life when he felt that way:

> "I know that nothing good dwells in me, that is, in my flesh; for the wishing is present in me, but the doing of the good is not. For the good that I wish, I do not do; but I practice the very evil that I do not wish. But if I am doing the very thing I do not wish, I am no longer the one doing it, but sin which dwells in me. I joyfully concur with the law of God in the inner man, but I see a different law in the members of my body, waging war against the law of my mind, and making me a prisoner of the law of sin" (Romans 7:18-20, 22, 23).

It seems to me that Paul was talking about his preconversion days in those verses, for he asked, "Who will set me free from the body of this death?" Then he answered his own question, "Thanks be to

Outside of Christ	In Christ
"I am no longer the one doing it, but sin which dwells in me" (Romans 7:20).	"It is no longer I who live, but Christ lives in me" (Galatians 2:20).
"A different law in the members of my body, . . . making me a prisoner of the law of sin" (Romans 7:23).	"It was for freedom that Christ set us free" (Galatians 5:1).

God through Jesus Christ our Lord" (Romans 7:24, 25). In Christ Jesus, Paul considered himself a free man.

Paul moved from the agony of imprisonment to the beauty of freedom, and he made it clear that freedom came from being in Christ and having the Spirit of life (Romans 8:2; Galatians 5:1). After conversion, he *could* live for Christ.

How is it that we must become free to live for God? Sin separated us from God. Without the life of God in us, we cannot live in the image of God. Fallen humanity is not bent toward God, but away from Him. Without God's Spirit, we do not have the equipment to live for God. For this reason, God promised that the Spirit would come to free us from this inability.

Let us look into the past to see God's plan more clearly.

The Law

Since man cannot live God's way without the Holy Spirit, how did the people of the Old Testament survive without becoming totally evil? God knew that Christ would be the only way to free man from sin; thus He planned to send Him. If the people had no guidelines whatever for living, they would be so perverted and evil when He came that they would not recognize nor want Him. So until that time, God established the law as a guardrail along the highway of life to keep at least one group of people aimed toward the arrival of Jesus on earth.

The Law As a Guide

The law helped the people to realize what it meant to love God and others. As long as a person stayed within the intent of the law, he could be involved in doing a loving kind of activities. Only that kind of person would be able to recognize the pure love that was demonstrated in the life of Jesus when He came to earth.

The law acted as a guide, leading man to Jesus who was love in person. Paul expressed this truth when he said, "The Law has become our tutor to lead us to Christ, that we may be justified by faith" (Galatians 3:24). The word "tutor," or "custodian," as some versions have it, referred to a slave who accompanied a child to his teacher so that he would not stray too far off the road, get lost, and miss his schooling. The bus driver performs that function today, so we might say the law was the "bus driver" for the Jews. The law kept the people from getting so far off the track that they would miss Jesus when He came. It hemmed people in. It provided guardrails to keep people heading toward Jesus.

The Law As an Accuser

The law also spelled out what sin was. It let the people know they were sinners, so they would feel a need to have a Savior.

Paul wrote, "Why the Law then? It was added because of transgressions" (Galatians 3:19). Further he wrote, "I would not have come to know sin except through the Law" (Romans 7:7). Paul explained that the law revealed sin for what it really is. The law was given "that through the commandment sin might become utterly sinful" (7:13).

Because of the law, the people would know without a doubt that they needed "something else." The law, however, could not give life (Galatians 3:21); it could not give man the ability to live for God. Only the Spirit of God within us can give us the freedom and the new life to *enable* us to fulfill the requirements of the law (Romans 8:4). To be specific, then, what exactly does the law require? Jesus and Paul agreed on this point. The law requires love for God and for others. Such love fulfills the law.

Jesus	Paul
" 'You shall love the Lord your God with all your heart, and with all your soul, and with all your mind.' This is the great and foremost commandment. And a second is like it, 'You shall love your neighbor as yourself.' On these two commandments depend the whole Law and the Prophets" (Matthew 22:37-40).	"Owe nothing to anyone except to love one another; for he who loves his neighbor has fulfilled the law. For this, 'You shall not commit adultery, You shall not murder, You shall not steal, You shall not covet,' and if there is any other commandment, it is summed up in this saying, 'You shall love your neighbor as yourself' " (Romans 13:8-10).

The Law As a Shadow

So was the law abolished when Jesus came? No; Jesus did not come to do away with the law, but to fulfill it (Matthew 5:17). He lived out, in a visible demonstration, what the law could only outline—love. Then He nailed the many burdensome ordinances of the law to the tree (Colossians 2:14), because He wanted us to be free to live in the bonds of love, no longer in the bonds of the law. The Law, then, was simply a shadow of the real thing (vv. 16, 17).

A Type of Slavery

When we are in Christ, we are freed from the bonds of the law: "But now we have been released from the Law, having died to that by which we were bound, so that we serve in the newness of the Spirit and not in the oldness of the letter" (Romans 7:6).

I wish we could believe that! Many of us still try to live under the law system. The law system sometimes has a way of making us think we are saved by our own efforts. We rely on ourselves to keep track of a bunch of rules. If we follow those rules, then we pride ourselves for what "we" are accomplishing. This is the arrogance of self-justification.

At one time Paul thought he was righteous because of his own efforts (Philippians 3:9). He thought he was blameless because he kept the rules so well (v. 6).

How many of us from time to time get caught up in thinking we will make it to Heaven because the list of our good points is longer than the list of our bad points? This kind of thinking hampers our growth into the likeness of Christ. We will begin thinking, "Why do I need to do more or grow? I'm okay now." This misses the whole point of freedom.

We are freed to grow, love, and live like Christ. Anytime we are satisfied with our present status, we will see no need to care for the needs of the people around us. Our freedom to expand will be lost; we will have become closed in, enslaved to "our" level of safety, enslaved to only those activities that make us feel secure.

The rich young man came to Jesus with a long list of the goodies in which he felt secure (Mark 10:17-22), but he was not free to love. He was enslaved to his list of rules.

The Paradox of Freedom

God has liberated us, enabling us to develop into the likeness of Jesus. We *can* mature into His likeness! Let us quit saying it is impossible.

God has freed us from sin, from spiritual death, and from the law. His freedom is the freedom to love. In Christ we are unshackled from human traditions that are not based on a clear "thus saith the Lord." That freedom, however, does not give us the right to disregard other people's feelings. *They* may still be hooked on certain traditions. "Take care lest this liberty of yours somehow become a stumbling block to the weak" (1 Corinthians 8:9).

Yet, here is a paradox. The Christian is free, but he is not independent. He is free from the Old Testament law, but he is dependent on the law of Christ. It is truth that sets us free (John 8:32), but being in truth cannot be divorced from abiding in Jesus' word (8:31). Jesus' word is the only content of the love we are to live out.

Receiving God's Spirit (new life) enables us to love purely, but we begin in this new life as mere infants. Many of our old ways cling to us. We want to love, but often do not know what constitutes love. That is why we have the New Testament writings. They guide and direct us into pure love for others. The ability we have to love (Holy Spirit) is combined with the direction of how to love (God's will revealed in the New Testament).

Why do we need direction when we have freedom? The freedom we have is not the right to do as we please, but it is the liberty to please God, to do what is right in His eyes. We are free to live God's way. With that freedom we look for and delight in directions and guidelines that show us God's way. We are also thankful for the ability to follow those directions. We want to live for Him because we love Him, not because we want to follow external laws.

Conclusion

The new freedom we have in Christ means service. We are freed to serve. Paul put it this way: "For you were called to freedom, brethren; only do not turn your freedom into an opportunity for the flesh, but through love serve one another" (Galatians 5:13).

What a fantastic combination! Freedom and service! But we are to serve through *love*. God has freed us to love. Let us discover what love entails.

Lesson Eight

LOVE THAT LIVES

Love makes the world go around. Love is a "many-splendored thing." Love is a much-used and a much-thought-about word. But true, satisfying love must have some mysterious ingredients, because few there be who find it. While everyone wants it, few seem to know where to look for it.

Christians have an edge on everyone else for discovering love's mysteries. For the Christian, life and love go together like a horse and carriage. Without love you cannot have Christianity, nor can you live it or teach it.

Love is one of the few words found in every book of the New Testament. Why? Because love is the mark of the new life that is within us. We can tell whether or not we are Christians by how we display God's love: "Little children, let us not love with word or with tongue, but in deed and truth. We shall know by this that we are of the truth, and shall assure our heart before Him" (1 John 3:18, 19). Paul made this connection between Christian love and Christian living when he said, "The love of God has been poured out within our hearts through the Holy Spirit who was given to us" (Romans 5:5).

Any description of love in the New Testament is a description of God's character. The apostle John equates "love" with God, in 1 John 4. "God is love," he writes (vv. 8, 16). It has been suggested that we could substitute the word "God" (or Christ) for the word "love" in Paul's great love chapter (1 Corinthians 13:4-6). This is how it would read:

God is patient;

God is kind;
God is not jealous;
God does not brag, and is not arrogant;
God does not behave in an ugly way;
God does not seek His own;
God is not provoked;
God does not keep bringing up a wrong;
God does not rejoice in unrighteousness;
God rejoices with the truth.

When Paul told us we are to grow into the likeness of Christ in all aspects (Ephesians 4:15), what specifically did he mean? He explains it in 1 Timothy 1:5: "The goal of our instruction is love from a pure heart and a good conscience and a sincere faith." In other words, we are to love as Jesus did then, and would today.

Jesus himself gave us that command. On the night He was betrayed He said, "I'm giving you a new commandment, that you love one another." Had He stopped there, it might not have sounded so demanding, but He added, "even [in exactly the same manner] as I have loved you, that you also love one another" (John 13:34). Now, that is tough! This means that I am to love you exactly the way Jesus would love you if He were here in my 5'8" body, and you are to love me just exactly the way Jesus would if He were here.

The Meaning of Love

Jesus went on to say, " 'By this all men will know that you are My disciples, if you have love for one another' " (John 13:35). What Jesus did *not* say may be as important for us to note as what He *did* say. He did *not* say: "All men will know you are my disciples if you (1) have the right name in front of your church building; (2) never miss the Lord's Supper; (3) pray before every meal; (4) always carry a New Testament." None of these activities is wrong, of course. I believe in and practice them; but Jesus said the way people are really going to know that I am His disciple is by my love.

Love means different things to different people. There are many different kinds of love, but we usually use the same four-lettered word to describe each of them. A man can say, "I love my car" or he can say, "I love my wife." But in each case he has a different kind of love in mind (at least, we hope so).

The Greeks had at least four different words that meant "love." Each of these words expressed a different dimension of love. Let us consider three of those words.

Eros love is a one-way love. It describes a person's selfish concern for himself. Whatever he does, he does for himself, for his own benefit. He does not care whether or not he helps another as long as he is benefited. This kind of love would be demonstrated by a person who gave money to a charitable cause just for the credit he would receive.

Philos love is a two-way love. It is the mutual and affectionate love between close friends. A person wants to contribute to his friend's life and have the friend in turn contribute to his life. Christians are to have this kind of love. God had this kind of love for Jesus (John 5:19, 20); and Jesus had this kind of love for God and for others (13:20; 17:21). It is the friendship kind of love.

Agape love (pronounced ah-GAH-pay) describes a person's unselfish concern for others. What he does, he does for the benefit of others with no thought for himself. This is the word Jesus used when He said, "Love as I loved." A person with this kind of love: (1) sees a need; (2) moves to meet that need; (3) does not count the cost; (4) does not consider what he will get out of it; (5) does not consider whether or not the person is worthy of being helped; and (6) makes decisions with the welfare of the other in mind.

Jesus said we were to love like this. Paul said that this kind of love was to be the goal of our instruction. Our teaching and fellowship with one another should be aimed at helping one another grow into that kind of love. How do we do this?

Growing in Love

First, we must be sensitive to the needs of others. This means we will have to slow down, spend time with people, and listen. Did you ever get the idea that Jesus was in a hurry? Many of us, on the other hand, seem to be hooked on rushing here and there. If we ever do slow down, we do not know what to do with ourselves. In this attitude, it is hard for us to listen to others.

Does the following sound familiar? While a friend is talking to you, you are thinking ahead about what you are going to say when he quits. Or sometimes you butt right in without waiting for the other to quit!

Second, we are to be aware of the fact that we must love our enemies as well as our Christian brothers and sisters. But unless we can love those inside God's family, we will not be able to love those on the outside. *Agape* love must be developed within God's family, so let us consider the needs of those within God's family.

Developmental Needs of a Christian

Although individuals have their own unique needs, all of us share some common needs. The needs of a new Christian are the same kinds of developmental needs that a new baby has. After all, a new Christian has experienced a new birth and is a new creation.

The first basic need of a baby is that of *fellowship*. The baby wants to be touched, held, and talked to. If this need is not met, the baby is more susceptible to physical diseases and will have trouble developing emotionally.

Clinical studies have shown that babies in some of the primitive tribal surroundings develop better than babies in the United States, even without the benefit of Simalac or Gerber's foods. Why? Because the tribal mother wants her baby, and she cuddles and loves him from the moment of his birth. During the first two years of his life, the child is hardly ever, if ever, away from his mother.

Some hospitals in this country are finally realizing the advantages of allowing the baby the fellowship of his family. The baby stays in the room with the mother, and the father comes and goes as he wishes. This is proper fellowship, not programmed alienation.

The first need of a new Christian is also that of close fellowship. He needs the warmth of Christian people who care about him, not a packet of information stuck under his arm. Too often alienation begins right after his new birth, sometimes even before his baptism.

It happens like this: The preacher has gone fifteen minutes overtime with his message, and we are fidgety. Then it is time for the invitation hymn. We think, "Oh, I hope we sing only one stanza. If we don't get out soon, the Presbyterians and Methodists will beat us to the smorgasbord restaurant."

Alas! We sing five stanzas, and on the last one, someone comes down the aisle. We think, "Oh, no!" Then we apologize to God for being so callous. "Maybe it will be just a transfer of membership." But it isn't. It is a confession of repentance and faith and a desire to be baptized at that moment.

After his baptism and after he has changed clothes, the new Christian comes out into an empty church sanctuary. We are already on our way to the restaurant, trying to remember the name of the person who came forward that morning.

Every new Christian needs to know that the family of God is glad he is joining them and is starting a new life with them. He needs to spend time with at least one other member of his new family during the coming week.

The next need a new baby experiences is that of nourishment. But what kind of food? Hamburger and French fries? What would happen if we crammed a hog dog down the throat of a new baby? Sure! He would choke to death! At this time, his system can handle only milk.

I wonder how many new Christians have choked to death because they were thrust into classes with mature Christians and given the same diet. Words such as "grace," "justification," "expiation," "propitiation," "sanctification" are hard to swallow.

Let's give our new Christians milk before we give them meat. They need a special class with instruction on Bible words, beliefs, and the work of the church. They could use a study of the life of Christ and of the book of Acts before chewing on the more advanced material.

Another basic need of a baby is that of *discipline*. We start spanking our babies' hands and saying "no" when they are just a few months old, because we are concerned that they develop rightly. New Christians also need discipline. From the very beginning we need to share with them that we care about their Christian growth, and that we will come to them with "well dones" and "no-nos." Most people will welcome this discipline, if they are told to expect it.

When an infant reaches the age when he tries to walk, he needs lots of *encouragement* to walk alone. When our child took his first step, what did we do? We probably clapped, smiled, and encouraged him. Did we shout at him when he fell on the second step or step on him? Of course not. We picked him up when he fell, and comforted him. Why? Because we loved him and were so pleased that he was trying to walk. We wanted to encourage him to keep trying.

A new Christian will stumble from time to time in his new life. How do we handle it? Do we talk about him and say we knew he wouldn't last? We should be glad he is trying, pick him up, and encourage him. Paul said, "Brethren, even if a man is caught in any trespass, you who are spiritual, restore such a one in a spirit of gentleness" (Galatians 6:1).

Another area of development with a small child is his learning to *talk*. How does he learn this intricate skill? By listening and imitating those who are close to him. Babies will talk using the words they have heard.

What are new Christians hearing around them which they will be imitating soon? Are they hearing criticisms of the preacher and the church program? Are they hearing gossip and bitterness? Are they hearing joy, gratitude, honor, and encouragement? The topics of our conversation will soon be the topics of their talk. Would that make us happy?

Needs of Growing Christians

Christians who can no longer be considered "new," but who are striving to be like Jesus, have the same basic needs that we have just discussed, but these needs must be met in somewhat different ways.

The growing Christian never outgrows his need for fellowship. He needs the encouragement and support of other Christians. He needs the continual association and the sharing of one another's joys and burdens. If he is ignored or made to feel he is not worthy to be loved by others, his growth will be stunted. If he isolates himself from the concern of others, his growth will no doubt be aborted. We all need other Christians who show that they care about us, and we all need to seek to meet the needs of our fellow Christians.

Growing Christians certainly continue to need

the nourishment of God's Word. Through intimate fellowship with one another we should be able to ascertain with some amount of accuracy the level of knowledge and understanding that our fellow Christians have. This in turn necessitates our evaluating continually the educational program of our churches. We need to make sure that the teaching is geared to each Christian's interests, needs, and level of understanding.

Discipline is an ongoing process. We will not stop needing discipline until we all have arrived at Christian maturity, the stature of Christ.

The walk of a Christian continues also. We all are constantly facing new, different, and difficult situations. In order to meet these situations as God would have us to, we still need the help, support, and encouragement—and sometimes comfort—of our fellow Christians.

A few years ago, two of our children fell asleep at an evening meeting. My wife, Julia, carried the older and heavier child; I carried the "light as a feather" smaller child. She fell to the sidewalk with our son in her arms.

When we got to the car, I told her, "Honey, from now on I will always carry the heavier child. That is probably what got you off balance." We can do the same sort of caring in our family of God. When we see a brother slipping in his Christian walk, we need to ask, "What burden is he carrying that I could help him with?" Paul said, "Bear one another's burdens, and thus fulfill the law of Christ" (Galatians 6:2).

The talk of a Christian is also a continuing concern, for what a person says reflects what he thinks. We must always be evaluating whether our talk is worldly or Christlike. Mutual dependence between Christians, practice in loving and serving, continual Bible study and prayer—all will help keep our talk what it should be.

Conclusion

As Jesus trained His disciples, He met all the needs that we have discussed: fellowship, nourishment, discipline, encouragement in the walk, and guidance in the talk. Jesus called them first of all to travel *with* Him. He taught them in *parables,* simple stories geared to their understanding. He *corrected* them when they were wrong, and *forgave* them when they strayed. He *helped* them carry burdens, and promised to be with them always.

He commanded His disciples to love one another. They were to abide in Him so they could love others as He loved all mankind. They were to bear the fruit of love and were to be united so this love could be shared (John 15, 17).

God's life and love are inseparable. Let us who share His life extend His love to one another.

PART TWO:

Practical Comparisons

Jesus: "Whatever the Father does, these things the Son also does in like manner."
John 5:19

Paul: "The life which I now live in the flesh I live by faith in the Son of God, who loved me, and delivered Himself up for me"
Galatians 2:20

The Christian: "You have been bought with a price: therefore glorify God in your body"
1 Corinthians 6:20

Lesson Nine

LOVE THAT BREAKS DOWN WALLS

A small boy was carrying another on his back who was just about as big as he. A passing gentleman was a bit startled and asked, "Son, isn't that too much weight to carry?" The lad replied, "Oh, no, Sir. You see, he is my brother!"

I suspect that Jesus would have replied in much the same way from the cross, if someone had asked Him, "Isn't the pain too much to bear?" Jesus would have answered, "Oh, no. You see, these are my potential brothers!"

Paul displayed the same attitude. "I endure all things for the sake of those who are chosen, that they also may obtain the salvation which is in Christ Jesus and with it eternal glory" (2 Timothy 2:10). But he was not only concerned for his Christian brothers. His love was as wide as Jesus' love. Jesus' love extended to all of humanity, even when it got Him into trouble, and so it was with Paul.

A Narrow Love

The Hebrew people were experts at narrowing down love. They built many barriers that corralled people into their own corners and kept them there. Prejudices were the norm of the day.

The Hebrews taught that a Gentile was subhuman. Hebrew children were reared calling "other" people by animal names: pigs or dogs. The Hebrews set up many social rules to prevent association with the Gentiles. It was taught that the dust from Gentile soil defiled Hebrew soil, because the Gentiles themselves were defiled. Therefore, Jews who traveled to Jerusalem from other countries had to shake off Gentile dust.

The prejudice of the Hebrews was so sharp that if a spot of heathen dust got on an offering, the offering had to be burned. Only those who live on a farm know the full significance of the loss of a bull for such a silly reason. Perhaps we city people could visualize the absurdity of such a practice more clearly if we think about what it would mean to us if we had to destroy our car because some pagan dust got on it.

A Jew would not help a stricken Gentile or Samaritan. This is why the parable of the Good Samaritan is so significant—a Samaritan helped a Jew! Orthodox Jews would not even travel through Samaria to get to Galilee. What a waste of energy! They would go many miles out of their way just because of petty prejudices.

A Jew would not eat with a Gentile. Jewish men thanked God daily that they were not Gentiles, slaves, or women.

The Racial Wall

Jesus tore down racial barriers. He spent time with the Samaritans. He never took the detour to bypass Samaria (John 4). He ministered to the Gentiles (Mark 7:26). He died, arose, and ascended for all races: "And I, if I be lifted up from the earth, will draw all men to Myself" (John 12:32). Jesus left His disciples with orders to evangelize *all* nations.

People saw in Jesus a comrade before they saw Him as the Christ, a friend before they saw a Savior. He associated with the unlovely and touched the untouchables. It was in this association that He first brought the good news that God loved them.

Many people, however, were offended because of Jesus' unorthodox associations (Luke 15:2); but the twentieth-century body of Christ (the church) is to continue this type of association today (John 17:18; 1 Corinthians 5:9-11).

A congregation that rejects people on the basis of external standards can hardly be a reconciling church, just as a standoffish God could hardly be a sanctifying God. It is folly to think we can evangelize those with whom we will not first associate or fellowship. The verbal "good news" will be garbled by the static of the visible "bad news" to "stay in your place."

Jesus crushed all human-made barriers on the cross. "For He Himself is our peace, who made both groups [Jew and Gentile] into one, and broke down the barrier of the dividing wall" (Ephesians 2:14).

How far does our love extend in the race issue? Do we stay away from the "dust" of the other race? Do we stay away from their homes? Would we have one of another race in our homes or eat with him in his? Would we stop to help one of another race? Truly following Jesus' actions and attitudes is tough.

Christianity is not lived out just in the sanctuary, but also in the street. If Jesus died to unite the races in the church (Ephesians 2), how can we split the church when it becomes integrated? Do we even allow our church buses to go through the black housing community?

This is not an easy problem to solve. It was many years before any of the apostles crossed the racial barrier in evangelism. They had grown up with their prejudices; it is not easy to overcome deeply ingrained prejudices. God was patient with them, but also persistent.

From Acts 1 to 8, only Jews were being evangelized. It may have been as long as ten years before the first Gentile was converted (who was, I suspect, the Ethiopian eunuch). His conversion, however, did not pose a threat to Christianity in Palestine because he left the country shortly afterward.

The Jews rightly understood God's demand for the fellowshiping of His children. They knew they must associate with whomever they evangelized. That fellowship was not just to be for one day, either. It was to be a social fellowship of brothers and sisters who were one in Christ and who cared for one another. Thus the Jewish Christians were very reluctant to evangelize a Gentile.

The Ethiopian eunuch was no problem because he did not stay for the fellowship. Today, hardly any one would criticize you for evangelizing a black hitchhiker, even if you stopped to use the church's baptistery to immerse him. Most people would think this was great. But there would be a different reaction if after his baptism he announced, "You know, you folks have been so kind. I don't really have anywhere to go and settle down. I think I will stay in this community, get a job here, and worship in this church." Just imagine how the people of the church would look and what they would say!

God knew this racial barrier had to be crossed, so He called a special man, who would be committed to teach and live the truth, regardless of the personal consequences. That man was Paul.

Paul was known as the apostle to the Gentiles. God called him (Acts 9) between the time the first Gentile (who did not stay) was evangelized (Acts 8) and the time the next Gentile (who stayed in the fellowship) was evangelized.

As Jesus' mission was to be "a light of revelation to the Gentiles, and the glory of Thy people Israel" (Luke 2:32), so Paul was "a chosen instrument of Mine, to bear My name before the Gentiles and kings and the sons of Israel" (Acts 9:15). Who extended that call to Paul? Jesus! He wanted His mission to continue.

We must realize that with his conversion Paul completely changed his feelings toward the racial question. Prior to his conversion, he was not open to the Gentiles. Stephen spoke of the care God had for people beyond the "holy land" (Acts 7), and Paul heartily consented to his death. Paul and Peter were both Jews, and of the two Paul admittedly was more steeped in Jewish tradition than Peter (Galatians 1:13, 14). We know of Peter's reaction to Gentile evangelism before his vision (Acts 10), so we must realize that Paul's feelings must have been even stronger before his Damascus-road experience.

Paul was the primary person to keep pushing for the crossing of racial barriers. Through evangelism the races were coming together in Jesus, so that in Antioch the first integrated congregation was organized. In *that* kind of church, the disciples were first called Christians (Acts 11:19-26).

Other Walls

Besides racial prejudice, there were other walls that the Jews used to keep other people "in their places." The rich and the poor would not cross the wall that separated them to associate with one another. Well people would have nothing to do with sick people. The Jews were taught that a sick person was an enemy of God who was being punished by his sickness.

There was a wall between the males and females. The Jewish male put down women by teaching that they were subhuman. There was the sinner/saint barrier. The "holy" people failed to care for the sinners. The Jews also hated the Romans, especially the soldiers who were occupying the land.

Each of these walls separated people who were "different." We know that even today it is easier to stick with those of our own kind. It is tough to try to cross barriers of long standing.

But Jesus showed us how to break down walls. He was rich because of His heritage, but He spent time in the homes of the poor. He was poor in earthly possessions, but He made friends with the rich. He was well, but He touched the sick. He was a male, but He elevated women. He was "holy" but He ate with sinners. He was a citizen of an occupied country, but He encouraged everyone to pay taxes to the government and He ministered to soldiers.

The apostle Paul also showed us how to break down walls. He was likewise concerned about the poor. He spent a great deal of time collecting an offering for the poor in Jerusalem (1 Corinthians 16:1 ff; 2 Corinthians 8, 9; Romans 15:25, 26). He was friends with the rich. Luke, the physician, was his traveling companion. He was a friend of the rich Philemon, but he pleaded the case of the poor slave, Onesimus.

Paul ministered to the sick (Acts 14:9-11). After his vision in Troas, Paul attended a women's meeting by the riverside and evangelized them. In fact, Lydia was a rich woman (16:13, 14). It has been suggested that because of her wealth, the Philippian church was able to send money to Paul time and again (Philippians 4:15, 16).

Paul was at ease with soldiers, especially those assigned to guard him at various times. He turned to them, not away from them (1:12-14). In Acts 13:1 we clearly see Paul's ability to work with different people. His fellow workers included one who now owned no property (Barnabas), a black man (Simeon), a foreigner (Lucius), and a friend of Herod's (Manaen). What a team! Paul consistently had people on his team who were different from him; they complemented one another in the work for Christ.

The whole book of Acts is largely the account of how Christianity learned to cross all human barriers. Much of it was done by Paul, who was imitating Christ in loving others as Christ loved them. He turned his back on no one, except those who wanted to beat him. He was a man for all seasons. He could say

Christ lived within him, then point to his actions and reactions as proof.

Nowhere are the broken walls more evident than in Romans 16. Notice the array of people he greeted. Paul greeted women (Phoebe, Priscilla, Mary, Junias, Tryphaena, Tryphosa, Julia), three slaves (Ampliatus, Phlegon, Persis), three Jewish Christians (Andronicus, Junias, Herodian) and several Gentiles with Roman, Greek, and Asiatic names. What a diversity! Paul really meant it when he said, "There is neither Jew nor Greek, there is neither slave nor free man, there is neither male nor female; for you are all one in Christ Jesus" (Galatians 3:28).

Application

Are we breaking down walls? The church of our Lord is to be that one group of people who react to other people differently because the group itself is different. We Christians should turn away no one. We have a new life—the life of God—and we must be demonstrating the love of God.

The church is to be the united family of God, living amid the disuniting feuds of men. The church is a new people for whom the old labels are to be no longer important to association, evangelization, or fellowship.

Breaking down walls is not easy, nor is it done overnight. We have the equipment of the Spirit and the example of the Savior to help us. Let us walk in Him, even in this area of associating with those who are different from us. Christians are to be actively involved in including others to live in God's family.

The old society will continue to pigeonhole people in accordance with external standards. But those in the new society must be willing to reflect the character of Jesus, who does not keep people apart, but brings them together. He replaces hostility with peace, strangeness with friendship; He makes joint-citizens out of aliens, and brothers out of enemies (Ephesians 2:13-19).

Let us consider how we are doing. Do we reach out to those of another race? Do we fellowship with the sick? How many physically handicapped do we have in our services? In our homes? Do we cringe if a woman gets into the spotlight? Have we invited the wealthy to our homes? Do we become friends with the riffraff, or do we associate with just those of our "own kind"? Prejudices must be eliminated if we are to love the way Christ loved. If we have respect of persons (differentiate), we commit sin (James 2:9).

We must pray as Jesus prayed for us, that His love abide in us (John 17:21, 26). We must pray as Paul did, that our love might increase (Philippians 1:9), and become as wide as Christ's (Ephesians 3:17-19).

Is our love as high as Christ's—filled up to the fullness of God? Is our love as long as His—reaching to all kinds of people? Is our love as deep as His—meeting their needs without counting the cost? *How is your love life?*

Lesson Ten

WOMEN THEN AND NOW

Women! Where do they belong in God's creation? The male-female rift has been one of the most difficult to overcome. It may well be the last barrier to stand between humans and prevent them from loving as Christ loved.

One of the first practical results of being in Christ is that we are to look at people from a different perspective. We are to view them through God's eyes. Paul emphasized this truth when he said that the initial step of living for Christ was to see people properly (2 Corinthians 5:16, 17).

But such a giant step that is! It is difficult to see people properly when we have grown up looking at them through the glasses of our culture. If our culture has taught us that a certain group of people is inferior, it is not easy for us to lay those glasses aside. The longer we wear them, the more difficult it is to see clearly without them (we think).

Putting aside the old, erroneous glasses is possible for us because we are new creatures in Christ. As new creations of His, we are to take on the ministry of reconciliation (2 Corinthians 5:18). To truly reconcile others to Christ, we must see them as Christ sees them. To see others properly, we must be in Christ more than we are in our culture.

It all happens through a process of growth in Christ. As infants after our new birth, we will hold onto the old glasses for a while. As we grow into Christ, with the help of the Scriptures and other Christians who will teach and guide us, we can learn to put the glasses aside. We can view others as God does.

Early Culture and Women

During every time in history, it has been difficult for mankind to see women through God's eyes. It was certainly very difficult in the first century because of the cultural glasses of the time. Women were belittled. Greek philosophers taught that women were not fully human. It was believed that they were only a notch above the animal world, and so were to be treated like property.

One of the most significant Greek philosophers taught that the only way a woman could become human was for her to become a male. Such teaching continued for a long time. In the middle of the second century someone claimed that Peter stated, "Women are not worthy of the Life," and that Jesus replied, "Every woman who makes herself male will enter the Kingdom of heaven" (from *Gospel According to Thomas*).

It was taught that women were inferior intellectually and were liars by nature. Many girl babies were drowned. If one escaped the drowning, she was likely to be the victim of a harsh divorce when she was older. In those days a woman was nearly as helpless facing a divorce as she had been facing a drowning. Men divorced them for burning the food, talking to a man in public, letting her hair hang loose, being unveiled, talking too loudly, making unkind remarks about her in-laws, and not looking pretty.

It was considered a disgrace for a teacher to talk with a woman in the street. Women were not welcomed at public meeting places. Some even felt women should stay indoors all the time.

Jesus and Women

Jesus failed to wear the glasses of such a culture. He maintained a high respect toward womanhood. He condemned men who lusted after women (Matthew 5:28). He called a halt to men divorcing their wives for such liberal reasons as previously stated (5:31, 32; 19:1-12). He told parables in which women had key roles (13:33; Luke 15:8). He fed hungry women as well as hungry men (Matthew 14:21). He commended the faith of women as well as that of men (15:28). He commended women for ministering to Him. He even commanded that wherever the gospel was preached the service of one woman should be included (26:10-13). This is a much-neglected command. Jesus never issued a similar command about a man's service to Him.

Jesus cast unclean spirits out of women as well as out of men (Mark 7:25; Luke 8:2). He raised women from the dead (Mark 5:35-43). Outside of the twelve apostles, two out of three of His closest friends were women (John 11:5). Jesus allowed women to follow Him from place to place and financially support Him from their earnings (Luke 8:1-3; 23:49). He allowed a woman to tell others (including men) about Him (John 4).

He allowed a woman to anoint Him for burial (Matthew 26:12). One of His favorite places to visit was the house of a woman (Luke 10:38). Jesus taught Martha that a woman needed more fulfillment than just being a worker in the kitchen (10:40-42). He commissioned women to tell the disciples that He had risen (Matthew 28:1-11; Mark 16:1-7; John 20:15-17).

Why did Jesus have such a high view of women? Because Jesus saw women through God's eyes, not the glasses of men.

God's View of Women

We cannot appeal to God's view in the Old Testament to prove that He thought women were inferior. In fact, God had not completed His creative work with the male until after He had created the female (Genesis 2:18 ff). He created not only the male in His image, but also the female (Genesis 1:27; 5:1, 2). He gave to both male and female, as partners, the garden responsibilities (1:28). God did not declare His creation as "very good" until after the woman was made (1:31).

Adam saw in his bride a companion, not a competitor (2:23). God saw in her someone man should cleave to and become one with (2:22-24). Although women committed the first sin, it was not woman who first committed murder; it was man (4:1-8). It was not woman who first lusted with sexual perversion; it was man (6:1, 2).

It was the decision of courageous women that preserved the lives of Hebrew men (Exodus 1:17). This met God's approval (v. 20). It was a woman who saved Moses (2:1-10).

God declared through the inspired writer of Proverbs 31 that an excellent wife is well-balanced, not a prisoner in her own home. She is to be valued above earthly treasure; she is trustworthy (not a natural liar, as some taught). She is good for her husband and not lazy. She deals in real estate and gets income from outside the home. She has civic interests and is involved in community benevolence. Yet she does not neglect her family or house because of her outside activities. She is attractive. Her husband praises her. She is hardly an inferior person!

God used female prophets, persons who were inspired to speak for God. There were Miriam (Exodus 15:20), Deborah (Judges 4:4), Huldah (2 Kings 22:14), and an unnamed one (Isaiah 8:3). Leading men came to these women prophets to hear the word of God (2 Kings 22:14-20). Deborah was chosen to become the judge of the entire nation. A judge in that day was the civil, military, and religious leader of the people. Barak would not go to battle without her! Some of these female prophets were even married at the time (Judges 4:4; 2 Kings 22:14).

God continued to use female prophets in the New Testament. Anna was a prophet who spoke to people about God (Luke 2:36-38). Philip, a man of "good reputation, full of the Holy Spirit and of wisdom" (Acts 6:3-5), had four unmarried daughters who were prophetesses (21:8, 9).

Paul's View of Women

How would we expect Paul to view women? Before his conversion, he wore the glasses of his culture and so held the traditional views of his ancestors. At that time he probably did not have a high view of women. He no doubt prayed the same prayer that all Jewish men did daily: "Blessed be God that hath not made me a Gentile. Blessed be God that hath not made me a slave. Blessed be God that hath not made me a woman."

After his conversion, Paul felt differently and would never again pray that prayer. Compare his teaching in Galatians 3:28:

Traditional Prayer	Truth
"Blessed be God that hath not made me a Gentile."	"There is neither Jew nor Greek."
"Blessed be God that hath not made me a slave."	"There is neither slave nor free man."
"Blessed be God that hath not made me a woman."	"There is neither male nor female."

Paul looked at women the way Jesus did. He declared that man and woman should not be independent of each other (1 Corinthians 11:11). He taught that unmarried women as well as unmarried men may have the gift of celibacy (7:32-34). He certainly never refused to allow women to serve the Lord. He recognized that some married women were prophets (11:5).

Paul started a church in Philippi through a women's meeting (Acts 16:11-15). He encouraged the older women to teach younger women (Titus 2:3-5). He insisted that older widows be cared for (1 Timothy 5). He called Phoebe a "servant of the church" (Romans 16:1). This was the same word that was used to designate deacons. I am not suggesting that Phoebe was a deacon like those mentioned in 1 Timothy 3, but evidently she was used by the church for some commendable service. Although we do not know what that service was, we know that she was a "helper of many" (Romans 16:2). At least ten of the people whom Paul commended in Romans 16 were women (eight were named).

Many people surmise that Paul was a woman-hater because of two statements he made: (1) "Let the women keep silent in the churches; for they are not permitted to speak" (1 Corinthians 14:34); and (2) "I do not allow a woman to teach or exercise authority over a man, but to remain quiet" (1 Timothy 2:12).

We must not read those two statements and ignore everything else Paul said about women, and all that the Bible says about women. If we do ignore the rest of the Bible, we would no doubt conclude that women were to simply shut up and remain quiet—no praying, no singing, etc.

I doubt very much that this was what Paul meant. Let us consider these statements under the widest context possible: the whole Bible, the immediate context, the historical situation, and the words used.

It is my understanding that Paul was *not* saying that a female could never teach a male. He was saying that a wife should not disrupt a worship service by asking her husband questions, and that a wife should not hold authoritative teaching over her husband. I say this because of these reasons:

1 Corinthians 14:34

1. The rest of the Bible does not put the woman in the silent chamber. Remember all of the female prophets mentioned before.

2. The greek word for "woman" is also the Greek word for "wife." There is no other Greek word for either designation.

3. The Greek words for "husband" and "man" are also the same.

4. Usually when Paul used the words "woman" and "man" in the same context, he was referring to "wife" and "husband."

5. Paul's discussion is clearly a wife-husband relationship, and is so recognized by all translators of verse 35: "And if they ["women" of v. 34] desire to learn anything, let them ask their own husbands at home." If "men" in verse 35 is translated "husbands," then "women" must be translated "wives."

6. The kind of speaking they are not permitted to do is the asking of questions. In 1 Corinthians 11, Paul allows women to pray and to prophesy (vv. 4, 5). I find no hint that this was done in private, while the activities of chapter 14 were done in public. Both are public, or why would he stress the woman's dress in chapter 11? A person was not given the gift of prophecy for private use, as chapter 14 made clear.

7. The teaching of 14:34 is that of not causing confusion in the meeting (see v. 33). Confusion was caused by people talking at the same time, because many thought they had the gift of prophecy, or tongues, or interpretation, or song. They did not wait for one another to use their respective gifts. They forgot that their speaking was to be for someone else's edification (14:12, 26). Therefore, Paul told them to speak one at a time.

8. To add to this confusion, wives were calling out questions to their husbands. The men sat in one area and the women in another. When a wife did not hear a speaker, she evidently asked her husband what was said; but because they were separated, she had to ask loudly. Paul was telling the wives to quit that practice, for it was adding to the confusion and detracting from the worship service.

1 Timothy 2:9-15

1. Here also, Paul was probably dealing with the husband-wife relationship. Compare the close parallel of this Scripture with 1 Peter 3:1-6:

1 Timothy 2	**1 Peter 3**
Dress (v. 9)	Dress (v. 3)
Behavior (v. 10)	Behavior (v. 4)
Submissiveness (v. 11)	Submissiveness (v. 5)
Appeal to Old Testament wife (v. 13)	Appeal to Old Testament wife (v. 6)

2. The woman (wife) is definitely to be submissive, which is substantiated by other Scripture (Ephesians 5:22); but she is not to be submissive to any man just because she is female and he is male. A wife is to be submissive to her own husband.

3. We read elsewhere in the Bible that women are teaching men (and some are married women). So how do we read 1 Timothy 2:12? Logically, we can read it only as referring to the husband-wife relationship. A wife can be the judge over the entire nation, but she is not to come home and exercise authority over her husband. He is to be the head of the home, even though she may be the head of a nation.

4. The word for "authority" is a strong word, meaning "to stand apart from another." This parallels the meaning of 1 Corinthians 11:11.

5. The example of Adam and Eve is clearly that

of husband and wife. The first family got into trouble when the wife acted independently of her husband.

6. The climax to this section was about the salvation of women through child-bearing (v. 15). Surely Paul was not suggesting that single women bear children! No, he was talking about wives. "To be saved" is probably not talking about eternal salvation, but about the wholeness of a woman. The wife will lose her womanness if she lives as the authority over her husband. The wife is not to bring up her husband, but her children. Her femininity will be preserved, providing that she continues to trust, love, and maintain self-restraint. A woman who dominates and bosses her husband loses her femininity; ultimately she will be the loser.

7. "To remain quiet" (v. 12) does not always mean "not to talk." The phrase comes from a word that can mean simply to have oneself under control. This meaning would fit in best with verses 11 and 15.

Summary

These statements of Paul mean that a wife is not to try to bring up her husband or to exert authority over him. She is to be submissive, she is to have self-restraint, and she is to bring up her children.

Application

I can hear those wheels turning now, ladies. I can hear you saying that Scripture does allow you the right to teach men. This may be true, but go slowly. A Christian does not demand or grab his rights. He does not cause offense to a brother. A woman should not teach a man in an environment where it is not accepted.

At the same time, if we hold to the old tradition that a woman must keep quiet and not teach *any* male, then we have to work through some other tough problems in order to be consistent:

(1) When is a boy a man?

(2) Does this apply to "only in the church"?

(3) When are we not in the church?

(4) How can we allow women to teach males all week in public high school, but then say it is sin for a woman to teach them for twenty minutes in Bible school?

(5) How can we allow women teachers in our Bible colleges?

(6) What about women writers of our literature?

(7) What about the fact that many of the editors in our religious publishing houses are women?

(8) How can we send women into the field to be missionaries?

(9) How can we allow women to teach in our Christian day schools?

(10) How can we allow female choir directors to teach music to males?

Could we go as far as to say a woman may be an elder or deacon of a church? No. She could not fill the qualification of being the husband of one wife (1 Timothy 3:2).

I understand that women as well as men are important members of the body of Christ and have God-given gifts (1 Corinthians 12; Romans 12; 1 Peter 4:10). I see no reason for either sex to feel superior or inferior in the church.

Let us recognize the mutual abilities we have. But also let us recognize the abilities and responsibilities that are different. Women, don't try to act like men. Men, don't treat women as if they were second-rate. We need each other. May we demonstrate unity amid our differences. Let us take off our cultural glasses, look at each other as God sees us, and break down the wall of separation between the sexes!

Lesson Eleven

SURVIVAL OF THE FAMILY

Can the American family survive? That was the question posed by the October 27, 1975, issue of *U. S. News and World Report*. What shocks are threatening the American family? There are many.

High Mobility. People are on the move. That is quite different from when I was a boy. From the time I was born until I entered military service, I lived in only two different houses. My mother is still living in the same house into which we moved in 1939. But our son, Randy, is living in a different time. He has lived in eight different houses in nine years. That is high mobility!

High Fragmentation. When I was growing up, I knew where I would spend each evening—at home. Our entire family was home. We did not have to plan special family nights, for every night was "family night." We needed only one car, because no one was going anywhere unless we all went together. We did not panic when the television broke down, because we did not have one. I never once wondered where my mother and father would be on a certain night. I knew they would be home. I never had a baby-sitter. We were a united family.

Today, however, families are very fragmented. The family members are scattered more than they are together. Have you noticed how the activities at work, the clubs, the church, and the school keep each member on a different schedule?

I would like to see the community declare war on such fragmentation of the family. The church should quit having different meetings every night of the week, further separating the family. School boards ought to demand that most school-related activities be conducted during school hours.

Lack of Communication. One researcher discovered that the average husband and wife spend only thirty-seven minutes a week talking with each other. Another found that the average father spends only three seconds a day in undivided attention with his children under two years old, and only one minute a day with older children.

What a tragedy! Too many children do not have their needs met in the most critical time of their lives. Much of the security of children is formed in certain times in each day. Consider these:

(1) When they get up. What environment awaits our children when they first get up? Rushing, yelling, arguing? Do they ever find someone who is happy to see them and can listen to their dreams of the night or their plans for the day?

(2) At mealtime. When all the family eats together, a bond is established that cannot be established in any other way. It is *so* important for the family to avoid eating in shifts!

(3) When they leave for school. Does anyone help the children get ready and give them a good breakfast? Does anyone see them off to school? In what attitude do they leave home? Are they mad, lonely, afraid, frustrated?

(4) When they return home from school. Who is there to greet them? Are there cookies and milk waiting for them? There are millions of "latch-key" children who return to empty houses after school to await their parents' return from work. Too often this idle, lonely time turns into *trouble!*

(5) When they get hurt. Is there someone at home who cares, comforts, and sympathizes? They will go to this same person for comfort throughout their lives, whether their hurt is physical or not. What happens when no one is there?

Children want their parents to be the ones to meet these needs. If parents are gone or are too busy when they are home, the door to communication and help is closed. It is little wonder that these same children, when they become teenagers, have difficulty in communicating to their parents.

(6) When they go to bed. Do they know that Mom and Dad are home, and do they feel secure in that knowledge? Do they feel loved? Do they get a good-night hug and kiss? Do they go to bed feeling happy, secure, and loved, or sad, lonely, and rejected or guilty?

High Economy. A bad situation of economics has frightened the members of the family into a strange pattern of living. They go to work at jobs they don't like, in order to buy things they don't need and won't last, with money they borrow and can't pay back, in order to keep up with people they don't know or like.

They come home to relax from such pressures, but can't. They take pills to wind down and more pills to wind up the next morning. No one has enough of himself left over to share with another.

High Competition. Parents are pushing to get ahead at work, and the children are pushing to get ahead at school. We all want to be on top. It is very hard for a family to be a loving community when each member competes with someone else all day.

On a recent plane trip, I read an airline magazine article on the high cost of success. The major thrust of the article was the great loss dealt to the family life of those who were constantly trying to get ahead.

Lack of Commitment. Because of all these other threats, family members are turning inwardly. There is very little unselfish commitment to another, and this is especially visible in American family life. In the past ten years, marriage has declined eight percent, while divorce has increased ten percent.

I truly feel that one of the major reasons for divorce is the lack of commitment between husbands and wives. We haven't committed ourselves to anyone anywhere else, and we don't at home either.

In this type of environment, it is difficult for children to develop the necessary qualities of determination, fulfilling responsibilities, or perseverance. It is hard for them to develop meaningful relationships with anyone. It becomes hard to cope with life if we do not have the security of being committed to others. It is no surprise that one million young people run away from home each year! It is no surprise that suicide is the second leading cause of death of young people between 15 and 25 years old. It is no surprise that abortion is legalized—that is legalized lack of commitment! It is no surprise that we have a better chance of being killed by a family member than by a total stranger!

These situations are all symptoms of a basic lack of commitment. Dr. David Mace, after interviewing many runaway children, determined that the major reason for running away was the poor quality of their parents' marriages. He concluded that the best setting for the proper development of children was to have parents who live together in a warm, loving, mutually supportive relationship. He said that there is no more precious gift that we can give our children than for husbands and wives who care for and respect each other, and are committed to one another and their marriage bond.

Jesus and the Family

Jesus taught that when we become adults we need to make decisions about Him regardless of our family ties (Matthew 10). In this chapter, Jesus was sending His twelve disciples into Jewish cities to teach the Jews what He had taught them. They would not be teaching Judaism to the Jews. What they were sent to teach would cause problems, internal family problems. A family member who changed to Christianity from Judaism could expect a negative reaction from the other family members. Jesus said *adults* were to make these decisions, not children. He was not advocating rebellion, however, as some have surmised.

Jesus knew that whoever gave his life to Him would find new life (10:39). Therefore, to love another family member truly is to allow him to follow Jesus. In our new life we are able to love our family members in God's way, whether or not they understand or appreciate our change of religion.

Jesus taught that children must never cease to honor their parents. Grown children are to honor their parents, not only by obeying them, but by respecting them and providing for their needs (15:1-9).

Jesus taught that commitment was essential. He taught that husbands and wives should be committed to each other. He expected husbands to leave their mothers and fathers when entering marriage. A husband was to cut the apron strings and be totally committed to his mate. Only when a couple truly leaves the parents, and each is totally dedicated to live for the other, can the pair become a team that God intends. They will be one (Matthew 19:4, 5).

Jesus declared that the practice of divorce must stop (5:31, 32; 19:1-9). He allowed divorce when adultery was involved. When it comes to remarriage after a divorce, Christians hold diverse views, for different understandings of Jesus' teaching are possible.

> "Each must continue to study and to allow his personal position to rest upon the teachings and understanding of God's Word, rather than our experiences in the traditions of the world. We must also relate to fellow Christians who hold positions that differ from ours. We must do this in the character of Christ and with His willingness to

minister to a person regardless of his status in life. An appeal to Jesus for remarriage after divorce rests more upon His love, mercy, grace, and forgiveness than upon the 'permissive' texts."[1]

God's teaching and intention is for marriage to create such a unit that to love one's mate is to love oneself (Ephesians 5:28). For either to cut off his mate is to cut off something of himself. So it was out of love for us that Jesus said, "Whom God has yoked together, no man must separate." (Matthew 19:6)

This points up the importance of the parents' allowing their grown children to leave. I have seen too many cases where a couple cannot cleave to each other because their parents keep calling the shots. This is the worst thing that parents can do to their children and grandchildren! Children need the security of seeing their parents committed to one another and becoming one. Only in this way can they themselves anticipate and enjoy married life the way it should be.

Paul and the Family

Paul also taught that commitment between husband and wife was essential. Neither did he approve of divorce (Romans 7:2, 3; 1 Corinthians 7:39). He even said that a separated couple should remain single so the door to reconciliation would always be open (1 Corinthians 7:10, 11). He outlined responsibilities for each member of the family (Ephesians 5:21—6:4; Colossians 3:18-21). He advocated, as did Jesus, that grown children must care for aged parents (1 Timothy 5).

All of Paul's ethical teachings must also be poured into our family living. In both Ephesians and

---

[1]Knofel Staton, *Home Can Be a Happy Place* (Cincinnati: Standard Publishing Co., 1975), p. 38.

Colossians, he first taught general ethical attitudes and actions; then he showed how they applied in family life. This was not by accident. The home is the first place where Christian living is to be found.

By applying the practical teachings of Jesus and Paul into our home life, we can indeed survive the shocks to the American family. The same conditions threatened the families of their day as they do ours.

Application

The fragmentation of our families is so serious that the church must do something about it. We must seek ways to help the family be together more. Here are some practical suggestions:

1. Plan more church-sponsored activities for the *entire* family. Quit segregating the youth and children from their parents all the time. Rent the roller-skating rink or the bowling alley for family activities. Have the family units make up the teams. Sponsor family games—softball, volleyball, etc.

2. Encourage family members to sit together in worship services at least once in a while. Don't let graded worship separate the family members all the time. Let them sit together one Sunday a month, or have the children sit with their parents until time for the sermon, then they could go to their graded worship. You should allow your graded worship workers to rotate their duties so husbands and wives can be together in worship some of the time.

3. Encourage husband-wife teams to teach in all phases of the educational system—Bible school, vacation Bible school, youth groups, etc.

4. Use family units for services—greeters, preparing Communion, ushering, taking up the offering. Let family members baptize other family members.

5. Plan a family retreat, but don't separate the family members. Let the whole family do everything together—go to classes, play, eat, pray, etc.

6. Encourage good family reading.

7. Have family units form committees.

8. Help the parents develop Christian education at home.

9. Encourage families to spend more time together, by suggesting possible activities from the pulpit and from the church paper.

Families cannot be eliminated, no matter how threatened. They are the foundation of the church and the community. On his ninetieth birthday, Will Durant, who had been married sixty-two years, said that his greatest concern was that the American family life had gone to pieces. He said, "If you get rid of the state, the family can maintain order; but get rid of the family and you have nothing."

We are all too busy or "involved" to improve our family life, but we can slow down if we want to. There is a poem in which a small boy says to his daddy, "Tomorrow I'll be big, but I'm little now. Now is when I need you." We may not have tomorrow. Let's find time for our families today!

Lesson Twelve

CHRISTIAN REACTIONS

A booklet entitled *Your Reactions Are Showing,* by J. Allan Peterson, reveals that our true selves are reflected more by our reactions than by our actions. We can plan and practice our actions, but our reactions are spontaneous. It is difficult to disguise our true selves when our reactions are showing.

What about our reactions as Christians? I'm sure you have had it happen time and again. You are driving out of the parking lot after the ball game, happy as a lark. Your team won! Then it happens. You hesitate just for a second to move into the traffic, so the car at your side edges you out of your slot. Now how do you react? Do you wave and smile, or do you say under your breath, "That smart aleck! I'll show him!" Suppose the light changes, and the guy behind you "lays on the horn" before you have time to press on the gas pedal. Do you "play turtle" for the next block just to show him who is boss?

Jesus and Paul have many teachings about our reactions. We will consider two of them.

Turn the Other Cheek

Of all the teachings of Jesus, this probably is the one that is most talked about and the toughest to put into practice. Our culture, especially television, teaches us that it is cowardly to follow Jesus' teaching in this area. Who wants to turn the other cheek (Matthew 5:39)?

A 1975 issue of *U.S. News and World Report* attributed television with being the principle influence of our moral values, moving ahead of the home, church, and school. The research revealed that by the time a child reaches eighteen, he has spent twenty thousand hours watching television. That is more time than he has spent in school. It was learned that TV violence occurred five to nine times an hour in prime time, and as often as thirty times an hour on the Saturday morning children's programs.

It is not just that the children watch it, but they see us adults enjoying shows in which people shoot, stab, and beat one another to death. This bombardment through such an effective medium teaches us that whatever another person does controls our reactions. "If a person takes advantage of you, get even. Whatever others do or will do to you, do it to them first." So teaches television.

Such a philosophy of life is in direct contradiction to the teachings of Jesus and Paul. Jesus never treated others the way they treated Him. When His disciple cut the ear off one of the men who came to arrest Him, Jesus restored the ear (Luke 22:51) and said, "Put your sword back into its place; for all those who take up the sword shall perish by the sword" (Matthew 26:52). This teaching would be hard to swallow, especially when people are coming at you with lethal weapons. It takes the most radical kind of trust in Jesus to heed this advice.

Who will take care of us if we do turn the other cheek? God will, that's who! Jesus himself did not fight back when He was attacked. Nowhere is His vulnerability better stated than in Matthew 17:12, where Jesus said, "Elijah already came, and they did not recognize him, but did to him whatever they wished." This referred to John the Baptist, who was beheaded, but Jesus added that the Son of Man would also suffer at their hands. Also, the false accusations, the scourging, mocking, spitting, and beating, as well as the crucifixion itself, were endured without retaliation. Even as Jesus suffered on the cross, His persecutors tried to get Him to take matters into His own hands. "You who destroy the temple and rebuild it in three days, save Yourself! If You are the Son of God, come down from the cross" (Matthew 27:40). In jest, they declared, "He trusts in God; let Him deliver Him now" (27:43).

In their mockery, they were entirely correct. Jesus did trust himself to God; and He did not react to them in the same way they were acting toward Him. Partly because of this strange reaction of Jesus, the soldier said "Truly this was the Son of God" (27:54).

Part of Jesus' teaching of the disciples was that they follow Him in His reactions. "Are you able to drink the cup that I am about to drink? My cup you shall drink" (20:22, 23). And indeed they did! All of the disciples were manhandled, but they did not manhandle anyone. They followed Jesus' example and exhortation to love, not only their neighbors, but also their enemies.

Paul also followed Jesus' example. His life was filled with opposition, but he did not fight back. He let people run him out of their cities, when he had the only message that could save them. Paul was roughly treated, persecuted, and slandered; but when he was reviled, he blessed; when persecuted, he endured; when slandered, he tried to conciliate (1 Corinthians 4:11-13).

Paul was imprisoned often, beaten more times than he could count. He was endangered because of robbers, because of Jews, and because of Gentiles (2 Corinthians 11:23-27); but he never lashed back. He could even write after such treatment, "Never take your own revenge, beloved, . . . Do not be overcome by evil, but overcome evil with good" (Romans 12:19-21).

Not only is this teaching difficult to practice, it is even illogical, if we listen to what our culture tells us. But let us be Christians and do it!

Does this mean we just sit around and do nothing? *No!* Jesus and Paul knew when to get out of a place (Matthew 12:14, 15; Acts 13:51). They challenged slander verbally rather than violently (John 18:19-24; Matthew 26:61-65; Acts 22-26; 2 Corinthians 10-12). They corrected the actions of others without watering down the truth (Matthew 22, 23; Galatians 2; 1 Corinthians 5). Paul appealed to his Roman citizenship when wrongfully treated (Acts 16:37-40). He asked for legal protection when he learned of a plot to kill him (21:31, 32). He appealed to Caesar when he learned of a possible frame-up (25:9-11). Both Jesus and Paul refused to take matters in their own hands and use physical violence.

Now comes the argument we always hear. You were just dying to use it, weren't you? "Would you just stand by and let someone beat your children and rape your wife?" I do not honestly know what I would do when in such a situation, but I would hope that I would not let someone's actions control my reactions. I do not feel that physical violence is the only option available.

Are we then to allow violence and terrorism to continue? *No!* Then how will it be stopped if we do not retaliate?

Render to Caesar the Things That Are Caesar's

The first question to ask when considering this teaching is, "Just what belongs to Caesar (government)?" The answer is taxes (Matthew 22:17-21) and punishment of evildoers (Romans 13:3, 4). Paul's teaching is that we should not take vengeance into our own hands, and he showed us one way that God exercises His vengeance: through the governmental authorities.

This is all well and good while the taxes are being spent the way we want them to be spent, and as long as the government is adequately bringing "wrath upon the one who practices evil" (Romans 13:4). But when our tax money supports evil practices and the government protects the evildoer instead of punishing him, what are we to do?

In responding to the government, there are two extreme approaches that we can take: stand opposed to it or deify it. Both approaches are wrong. It takes radical trust to refuse the revolutionary approach and live in submission to the government with the belief that as vengeance against individuals belongs to God, so does vengeance against nations. It is not for the Christian to take either into his own hands and use violence. Rather than to prey upon the government, we are to pray for it (1 Timothy 2:1-3).

While our taxes and punishment to evildoers belong to our government, our trust and obedience belong to God. Human authority is never to replace divine authority (Romans 13:3-5). When human authority violates its purpose under God, it perverts the reason God established it. The highest authority is always God (Acts 4:18-20).

The Christian must be willing to take whatever consequences are coming when he obeys God rather than the government. This takes radical trust, but it is this kind of trust that demonstrates to the world that Jesus is Lord.

At the same time, we do not have to be obnoxious. We must be flexible. Jesus told His disciples to be flexible before sending them into the Greek culture, to eat and drink "what they give you" (Luke 10:7). Paul taught that same freedom (Romans 13; 1 Corinthians 8, 9; 10:27).

We can live in a community with the customs of that community becoming our own, if in doing so we do not disobey God's express commands. As Christians move from community to community, or from country to country, they must demonstrate that they can live in the world without being *of* the world.

As one government replaces another, let us show that we are bigger than any governmental system. We can live under any government as long as we are not asked to disobey God. Let us develop radical trust displayed by both Jesus and Paul that allowed them to be citizens of their generation without losing citizenship in the eternal generation. A writer in the second century saw the life of the Christians in this way:

> "For the Christians are distinguished from other men neither by country, nor language, nor the customs which they observe. For they neither inhabit cities of their own, nor employ a peculiar form of speech, nor lead a life which is marked out by any singularity . . . nor do they like some proclaim themselves the advocates of any merely human doctrines. But inhabiting Greek as well as barbarian cities, . . . and following the customs of the natives in respect to clothing, food, and the rest of their ordinary conduct, they display to us their wonderful and confessedly striking method of life . . . as citizens they share in all things with others . . . They are in the flesh, but they do not live after the flesh. They pass their days on earth, but they are citizens of heaven. They obey the prescribed laws, and . . . surpass the laws . . . They are insulted, and repay insult with honor . . . They do good . . . they love all men . . . Those who hate them are not able to assign any reason for their hatred . . . To sum up . . . what the soul is in the body, that are Christians in the world."[1]

May the same be said of Christians today.

---

[1] *Ante-Nicene Fathers*, Vol. I, pp. 25, 26.

Lesson Thirteen

CHRIST'S VIEW OF GREATNESS

"Daddy, before I tell you what I want, will you say yes?"

Have you ever been so questioned? It is comical at first thought, but underneath the surface there is a bit of tragedy in that kind of request. First, any personal responsibility on the part of the questioner is dodged. The implication is, "Do as I ask, with no strings attached." Second, the person asking doesn't really believe his request will be granted unless the other person agrees to it ahead of time. Once committed, he can hardly refuse.

What does the average parent answer when he hears such a request? If he is wise he says, "Wait a minute. I'm not saying yes or no until I hear what you have in mind."

That was the same tone as Jesus' answer when James and John made such a request of Him (Mark 10:35, 36). They didn't ask for much, or did they? They simply asked to be the two greatest guys in Jesus' kingdom (Mark 10:37)! It would be nice to have greatness just for the asking.

The problem was they wanted to jump to greatness by dodging the route to greatness. They wanted to be *declared* great. But Jesus made it clear that greatness is not a matter of *declaration,* but a matter of *demonstration.*

What kind of demonstration of greatness did Jesus mean? Too often greatness has been sought by grabbing the limelight and stepping on others. Jesus rejected that approach in His own life and He rejected it in His teaching.

Route to Greatness

In two sentences, Jesus describes the way to greatness: " 'You know that those who are recognized as rulers of the Gentiles lord it over them; and their great men exercise authority over them. But it is not so among you, but whoever wishes to become great among you shall be your servant; and whoever wishes to be first among you shall be slave of all' " (Mark 10:42-44).

Jesus did not criticize people for wanting greatness, but they must become great in the right way. It is not by pushing or pulling, or bullying their way to the top. No, it is the servant who is great, and it is the slave of all who is first. Being in another's spotlight is neither the route nor the goal of greatness, but being at another's service. Greatness is not demonstrated by living as lords over others, but as servants under them. Jesus also said that *He* was the way, "For even the Son of Man did not come to be served, but to serve" (10:45). He is our best model for greatness.

The Biblical route to greatness always follows the same pattern: from honor, to humility, to honor.

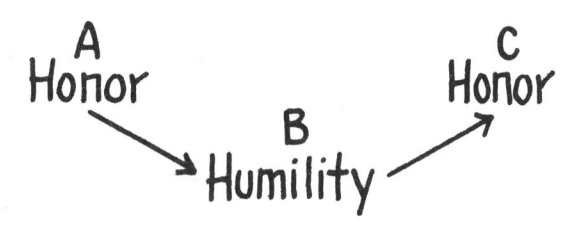

```
   A                        C
Honor                    Honor
         B
      ↘ Humility ↗
```

While some try to move directly to honor through self-assertion, Jesus both taught and demonstrated that we are to move to honor through humility.

In his Gospel, John showed the route to greatness that Jesus followed:

(A) "In the beginning was the Word, and the Word was with God, and the Word was God" (1:1).

(B) "And the Word became flesh, and dwelt among us" (v. 14).

(C) "And we beheld His glory, glory as of the only begotten from the Father, full of grace and truth" (v. 14).

Jesus spoke about this route to greatness several times. In Mark 10:33, 34, He spoke of himself as (a) the Son of Man, being (b) condemned to death, but three days later (c) rising again.

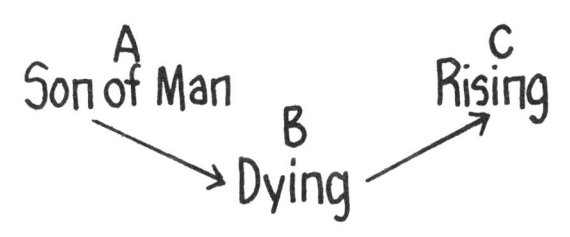

```
        A                        C
Son of Man              Rising
              B        ↗
              ↘ Dying ─
```

Paul understood the route to greatness in the same way:

(A) "He existed in the form of God" (Philippians 2:6).

(B) "But emptied Himself, taking the form of a bond-servant, and being made in the likeness of men ... He humbled Himself by becoming obedient to the point of death, even death on a cross" (vv. 7, 8).

(C) "Therefore also God highly exalted Him" (v. 9).

Jesus made it clear to James and John that they too must follow this route to greatness. He was suggesting that fact when He first commanded, "Follow me."

Paul also made it clear to his readers that all Christians must follow Jesus' way to greatness: "Have this attitude in yourselves which was also in Christ Jesus" (2:5).

We cannot bypass servanthood and expect to share in Christ's exaltation. Now let us consider what is specifically required of servants.

The Right Attitude

A very necessary attitude for one who is to be great is that he feels that he is not great in and of himself. A person puffed up with thoughts of himself is too "psychologically fat" to serve another.

Pride, a major topic in the Bible, prevents a person from correctly seeing himself, God, and others. Jesus said that pride defiles a person (Mark 7:22, 23). He frequently told people to get their heads out of the clouds.

Pride prevents one from being teachable, which in turn may cause storms among God's people. Paul connected pride with controversies (1 Timothy 6:4).

Isn't it interesting that Jesus, who knew more than all of His teachers by the time He was twelve years old, continued to attend the synagogue regularly? With all of His knowledge, He did not become puffed up. He saw the value in sitting under others. And what about Paul, who knew far more than the Roman Christians, yet he looked forward to being encouraged by them (Romans 1:12)?

What about us? How open are we to another if he does not have as much education as we have, or if he goofs in his grammatical usage? Do we look for the contribution he makes, or do we just look for his mistakes so we can zap him?

Pride also prevents a person from giving his life in service for others. The Corinthians were severely criticized for their arrogance. Their fellowship was disrupted because they had a tough time helping the other person.

I wish we could all understand what it means for us to be of service to another. Can you imagine how wonderful it would be if God would say to you on Judgment Day, "You have been a helper to children, to the aged, to the poor, to the rich, to the sick, to the preacher, to the custodian, to parents, and to your fellow workers"?

Perhaps helping our fellow workers is the hardest, for if we help them, they may rise above us. Do we want others to succeed? Can we decrease as they increase?

Pride also prevents a person from giving another credit. Jesus and Paul both knew how to do that (Matthew 11:11; 26:12, 13; Romans 16).

The greatest service is doing good with no thought of getting credit or recognition. Some serve so they will be recognized and praised. Their "sacrifices" have turned into ego trips. Jesus' type of greatness calls for serving in order to help others, not to achieve greatness.

What about us? Does it "get our goat" to honor someone else? An attitude of servanthood involves thinking that others are more important than we are (Philippians 2:3).

The Right Activities

The activities of a servant of Christ are designed to please a neighbor, not self (Romans 15:2). They are using our gifts for another (12:4-6); associating with the lowly to benefit them (v. 16); refraining from quarreling over matters of opinion (14:1 ff); striving with one another, not against one another (15:30); looking out for other people's interests (Philippians 2:4).

Serving is willingness to go out of your way to please others (Colossians 3:12-23); restoring a fallen brother (Galatians 6:1); carrying each other's burdens (6:2); protecting another from mistreatment or misunderstanding, teaching a person about the need for salvation, and meeting physical needs whenever they arise.

There are many great people about whom we have never heard. They are moving about in their communities as light and leaven. They are not beating their own drums. They are not sending news releases about their work to the church paper. They simply help others from day to day.

Greatness Begins at Home

Some of God's greatest people are those mothers and fathers who stick with their kids through thick and thin, who know what it means to wipe away both physical and spiritual tears, and who know what it means to sacrifice without a word of thanks. They know what it is to watch over a sick body, losing sleep and being willing to be contaminated themselves. They have listened to heartaches and joy; they have had their hearts broken, but are still willing to forgive. They have felt the ache of loneliness; they have loved a retarded or crippled child; they have cried while others may not care. They have stored things in their hearts that their children will never know.

Greatness? It is living for the good of others without caring who gets the credit. It is the willingness to die a little so another can live a lot.

Conclusion

Jesus and Paul were the epitome of greatness, yet they did not live for that. They lived for God and for others. There was no contradiction between their teaching and their living. They replaced sin with service. They lived for the salvation of others and demonstrated the freedom available in the Holy Spirit. Their love was as wide as the needs of people; they crossed barriers that no one else would. They looked at people the way God did and called us to react—even in our families—as God would.

Do you want to become great? Then be great at home first. Do not lord it over another, but serve each other. Let us be servants everywhere. That is Jesus' way, and that was the way Paul lived it. Let us be known as people of "the Way" (Acts 19:9, 23).